At once provocative and inspiring, *Against the Flow* is a work of polemic from an internationally respected writer and thinker on arts education. Peter Abbs argues that contemporary education ignores the aesthetic and ethical as a result of being in thrall to such forces as the market economy and managerial and functional dictates. He identifies the present education system as being inimical to creativity and authentic learning and, instead, narrowly focused on the quantitative measuring of results. This absence of a creative and ethical dimension in education has implications for art making in wider society. Art is shown as emerging from, and appealing to, the ironic, postmodernist sensibility and mass media-led culture, while being devoid of philosophical significance.

Against the Flow opens up a fresh and timely debate about the vital power of creativity in modern education. Drawing on examples from modern poetry, literature and visual art, it is an eloquent and passionate argument for the need to develop ethical and aesthetic energies to confront the growing vacuity of contemporary culture.

Peter Abbs is Professor of Creative Writing, and formerly Professor of Arts Education, at the University of Sussex. He is an established poet who has written extensively on the role and importance of the arts and creativity in education.

Against the Flow

Education, the arts and postmodern culture

Peter Abbs

Routledge
Taylor & Francis Group

LONDON AND NEW YORK

First published 2003
by Routledge
2 Park Square, Milton Park, Abingdon, Oxon, OX14 4RN

Simultaneously published in the USA and Canada
by Routledge
270 Madison Ave, New York NY 10016

Routledge is an imprint of the Taylor & Francis Group

Transferred to Digital Printing 2008

Typeset in Palatino by
Keystroke, Jacaranda Lodge, Wolverhampton

British Library Cataloguing in Publication Data
A catalogue record for this book is available from the British Library

Library of Congress Cataloging in Publication Data
A catalog record has been requested

ISBN 0–415–29791–5 (HB)
ISBN 0–415–29792–3 (PB)

For
David Evans
in friendship

For all the world's sake something must be done. Those who have these disturbing thoughts must begin to do some of the neglected things. Even if it just be anybody, by no means the most suitable person. There is no one else at hand.

Rainer Maria Rilke in *The Notebook of Malte Laurids Brigge*

Contents

Plates

The following appear between pp. 84 and 85.

Acknowledgements

I wish to thank Julia Martin-Woodbridge for her labours in converting an untidy script into a formatted disk ready for the publisher. Once again, I am indebted to her for her reliable and positive support. An earlier version of Chapter 1 appeared in *The End of Knowledge in Higher Education* (1996) edited by R. Barnett and A. Griffin, London, Cassell. An earlier shorter version of Chapter 5 appeared in *The Self on the Page* (1998) edited by Celia Hunt and Fiona Sampson, London, Jessica Kingsley.

Illustrations

Plate 1   Samuel Palmer, *Self-portrait with Aureole* (*c*. 1826–27). Collection: Kerrison Preston.

Plate 2   Max Beckmann, *Self-portrait with a Glass Ball* (1956). Private Collection.

Plate 3   Vincent Van Gogh, *Self-portrait for Gauguin* (1888). Cambridge MA, Fogg Art Museum.

Plate 4   Frida Kahlo, *The Broken Column* (1944). Dolores Olmedo, Mexico City.

Plate 5   The medieval world-view, from the *Liber Divinorum Operum* of Saint Hildegard of Bingen. The Lucca Manuscript (*c*. AD 1200).

Plate 6   Image of Carl Jung's first mandala. Jung Estate, Baden, Switzerland.

Plate 7   Portrait of Marcel Duchamp, photograph by Alexander Liberman.

Plate 8   Andrzej Jackowski, *The Vigilant* (1984). By permission of the painter.

Plate 9   Andrzej Jackowski, *Toxic Tank* (1996). By permission of the painter.

Plate 10   Andrzej Jackowski, *The Boy who Broke the Spell* (1996). By permission of the painter.

Plate 11   Mary Lloyd Jones' great grandmother's quilt. Between 1850–1900. By permission of the painter.

Plate 12   Mary Lloyd Jones, *Cwm Rheidol* (*Scars*) (1993). By permission of the painter.

Plate 13   Mary Lloyd Jones, *Barclodiad y Gawres* (*The Goddess with an Apron-full*) (1988). By permission of the painter.

Plate 14   Harold Mockford *Night Ferry* (1999). By permission of the painter.

Plate 15   Harold Mockford *Waiting to go* (1994). By permission of the painter.

Plate 16   Harold Mockford *The Ancestors* (1993). By permission of the painter.

Plate 17   John Meirion Morris *Modron* (1996). By permission of the sculptor.

Plate 18   John Meirion Morris *Bran* (1993). By permission of the sculptor.

Plate 19   John Meirion Morris *Trywerin Monument* (1997). By permission of the sculptor.

Plate 20   John Meirion Morris *Trywerin Monument* (detail) (1997). By permission of the sculptor.

Introduction

This book is called against *Against the Flow* because its aim is to resist, as creatively as possible, some of the dominant tendencies of our time. Over the last two decades our educational system has come to resemble a broiler house regulated by managerial and functional dictates – a place devoid of creative energy and animating spirit. The flame of authentic learning has been snuffed out while in the society at large, with memorable exceptions, the nature of art-making has become narrow, professional, cynical and, invariably, devoid of philosophical significance. As soon as one raises issues relating to the spiritual, the aesthetic and the metaphysical, one is painfully aware that one is using a language that sounds almost offensive and, at the same time, addressing a context of radical depletion, that one is talking against the status quo of the national curriculum, against the drive of the consumer society and against the sensibility of postmodern intellectual fashion. In brief, that one is struggling against the flow.

In such a predicament one has to make a decision: to be quiet and withdraw or to speak out, but one knows that if one decides to speak out, then, one must do so with as much courage and directness as one can muster. I have decided, with some fear and trembling, on the latter course.

In this book I raise, above all, the neglected question of *meaning*:

What should education serve?
What should art serve?
What is culture for?

And I envisage these three questions as inextricably interrelated – as part of a single constellation relating to the question of understanding and developing life, of establishing a form of life-wisdom – again, in an age of mass certification, mass consumption and mass culture, an uncomfortable, an uneasy, a dissident concept. The chapters that follow are attempts to excavate aesthetic and metaphysical concerns which the dominant society has largely suppressed. What, I want to ask, has been left out? What has been excluded in our high-tech postmodern culture and its increasingly bureaucratic educational system? So much learning these days eschews any connection with individual life or creativity. In our schools and universities we have become pathologically obsessed with quantitative measurement rather than the qualitative flow of meaning, with a brute collective standardization rather than with more subtle modes of individuation. We must consider, in particular, three significant suppressions in the life of consciousness.

First of all, there has been a suppression of the spiritual and transcendent. Because, under the diffuse influence of postmodernism, all meanings have been relegated to language games – to 'the play of the signifier' as it is often called – a sense of broader collective significance has been lost. Our cultural world has shrunk to rhetoric in the intellectual sphere and to advertising and spin in the commercial world and, as the two spheres draw closer and closer together, we are left only with signs signifying little beyond their own stylistic flourish and the crass reign of brand-names. We need to know, then, whether in specific contexts of learning and art-making we can actively reclaim the power of the numinous, the power of the imagination, the power of those meanings which fulfil and encompass. I argue that such reclamations are still possible. I argue, for example, that we need to link the study of literature, once more, to the quest for wisdom and that a concept of the spiritual can still inform our understanding of education. However, the forms that wisdom and the spiritual may take will be different from what they were traditionally. The concept of spirituality proposed is emphatically post-Christian. Being against the flow is not a matter of piously advocating past practices and traditional canons; it is, rather, a matter of keeping open a creative connection with the best of the cultural past and taking its collective energy forward along radically different routes from those shaped by the twin powers of eclectic consumerism and electronic technology.

Second, there has been a suppression of values connected to the common realm: the loss of a sense of human solidarity and the virtual loss of those archetypes, traditionally animated by Christianity, relating to birth, love, labour, death and transformation, archetypes which can bind a society together poetically. A compassionate tolerance for difference has emerged, yes; but what has gone is an informing sense of what holds life together beyond the consumer imperative. Our materialist society, based on infinite simulation and stimulation, suppresses such subversive and, potentially, redeeming insights or, where it allows them in, debases them by brazenly linking them to brand names. 'Coca-Cola – the universal multicultural drink!' Authentic art, not advertising, should play a special role here restoring us to our deeper humanity; though much contemporary art has, in truth, become merely an adjunct to media hype and tabloid razzmatazz.

I will argue for a poetics of culture which resists any easy amalgamation with the status quo and which sees the function of the poet and the art-maker as all but shamanic, as one of challenging, subverting, transforming and healing. In poetry I will argue for an engaged poetics committed to restoring a connection between the word and the world, between the body and the imagination. In the visual arts, I will make a related argument, against conceptualism, for figurative and visionary art.

Third, there has been the loss of any binding notion of ethical or aesthetic value. In postmodern consumer societies most ethical and aesthetic judgements tend to be seen as absolutely relative – and, most often, merely subjective. Tellingly, 'discrimination' has become an entirely negative word and so has the ubiquitous 'judgemental' – a word which has come to denote the unwarranted imposition of one perspective over another, a matter of interfering power rather than a matter of precise discernment. Yet if all judgements in life are absolutely equal, nothing can matter. An egalitarianism in ethics and aesthetics is a manifestation of nihilism; it can offer no defence against the armed thug, the dictator or the advertising industry. That judgements relating to art and life can be extremely difficult to make is another matter.

And yet, tragically, we are losing the very language in which serious ethical and aesthetic reflection can take place. What we find increasingly in educational documents is a functional discourse which makes the educational status quo appear as the only conceivable reality. The sense of possibility, of ethical choice, is thus entirely erased. *Education becomes merely the sum total of current practices.* This is the subtle tyranny of instrumental pragmatism. Against this insidious trend which turns education into a species of social training serving the status quo, this book is written to defend the socratic play of meaning, the power and pertinence of ethical judgement and aesthetic discrimination. Indeed, the original concept of education bears within it a profound ethical import; it implies that some things are better than others (to be educated is better than not to be educated) and that one can move forward from one level to the next in some form of developmental sequence, however erratic. This is a seminal conception at the very heart of my argument.

It is perhaps inevitable that, at times, my words may baffle and mislead. I have chosen a poetic and philosophical language to pit against the anodyne and functional language of current educational discourse. I hope that in the specific contexts of each chapter my meanings will become clear to my reader; but there are two words that are especially difficult and I would like to comment on them here. As the most contentious word must be *metaphysical*, let me take that first.

Traditional metaphysics was, largely, confined to logical propositions and to the elaboration of complex systems of understanding, often essentialist or supernatural in character. In the former case, metaphysics was linked to versions of philosophical idealism and rationalism; in the latter with theology and doctrinal speculation. The word metaphysical in this book has virtually no connection with these grand narratives of explanation. I use the word to refer to a primary engagement with the making of meaning, with the search for understanding, with the desire for an encompassing sense of life. My assumption is that in a postmodern age the word metaphysical has to shift its meaning so that it refers not so much to those impossible systems of ultimate explanation but more to the process of questioning and questing which lie behind them. Metaphysical in these pages refers to the dilemmas of consciousness, to the open predicament of being human, a predicament which requires a creative response.

This brings me to the terms *postmodern* and *postmodernist*. By *postmodernist* I refer to those thinkers who adopt, in the famous words of Lyotard, 'incredulity to all meta-narratives'[1] and who allow in their thinking no space for universals or essences of any kind. It is, furthermore, a philosophy which generally invites a stance of irony towards experience. My approach, as my reader will have already gathered, does not conform to this position. Yet much of it is *postmodern*; and by postmodern here I refer to a recognition of the broken nature of our experience, the end of large explanatory 'isms', a sense of the incorrigible plurality of things, the demise of orthodox Christianity, and the need for a radical openness and bold creativity before the huge uncertainties of life. My general position towards postmodernism is one of ambivalence: I endorse some of the relativist philosophy while postulating some universals and I distrust the protective irony which marks its sensibility. I am also conscious of the failure of most postmodernists to engage *critically* with some of the most urgent questions posed by a global consumer culture. But this is to anticipate . . .

To conclude, I would like to make a few points about the organization of the book. I have divided it into two sections: Part 1, *The poetics of education*, and Part 2, *The poetics of culture*. This is a crude division which has only a rough justice. Readers interested in the arts in education would do well to turn to the first half of the book; those interested in the arts in the wider culture – literature, autobiography, poetry, the visual arts – to the second half. And yet, in truth, there is enormous overlap between the sections – for, as I have implied, I see authentic education and authentic culture as different expressions of the same quest for understanding and symbolic expression. This means that themes recur in both parts, that points made in one section are further elaborated in the next and so on. Indeed, I would prefer my reader to see the work as a loose fabric, a collage of related explorations, rather than a consecutive and cumulative narrative. Readers are invited to enter where they will and to follow the lines of their own passions and concerns.

I have prefaced each chapter with a short autobiographical prelude. Nietzsche once claimed that all philosophy was 'the confession of its author and a kind of involuntary unconscious memoir'.[2] Later this became a psychoanalytic insight into the personal nature of cognition and theory. *All seeing is perspectival.* I think there is considerable truth in this. The point of the brief personal prelude, then, is to bring out consciously the autobiographical connections with the argument that follows. It is also an attempt to put into practice what I have preached to my students at the University of Sussex over the last twenty years: begin where you are, think out of your existence, there is no need to hide.

Part I

The poetics of education

Chapter 1

The arts, postmodern culture and the inner dynamic of authentic education

I live near Beachy Head in Sussex. Some times I go down the cliffs at Birling Gap just to gaze up at the towering cliff face. It rises vertically up from the flat level of the sea like a white cathedral. It is all but sublime, tipped by the distant wings of gulls at the top and washed by the breaking waves of the sea below. At times, I wonder about the material of chalk. What exactly is it made of? How was it thrown up out of the sea and in what period of geological time?

I studied A level geography but was entirely indifferent to it and in the final examination received the lowest possible mark – a grade 9, less than 10 per cent. A disgrace. But now I can see why I wasn't interested and why Mr Edwards despaired of me. Never once did my tireless and well-meaning teacher engage my feelings, the latent energies of my aesthetic and existential responses. So I wasted his time and my own. Thus today when I look up at Beachy Head I still know virtually nothing about chalk, geological time and the forces behind the creation of this great natural beauty.

No existential engagement, no deep learning. This chapter is essentially about this neglected educational axiom. But it is also about the collaborative and dialogical nature of learning. It is concerned to make visible the often overlooked connections between – where it exists – the good classroom and the good society, between the creative school and the creative society. Most of the educational changes made during the last two decades under the nationalized curriculum have engineered a vast prescriptive system of convergent learning ('delivery of the curriculum' being one of the most tired and fatuous slogans ever conceived) at the expense of the potential creativity of the overloaded learner.

Pupils and students are now driven through a series of preconceived programmes to emerge as convergent members of the consumer society; I would rather have them go through a series of transformative experiences

*to enter a cultural democracy as reflective citizens and radical
contributors to the workplace.*

*There should always be time to gaze in speculative wonder at Beachy
Head before storming into the geography lesson with some passionate
questions grounded in one's own animating responses.*

*Mr Edwards wherever you are today – and today, because of national
policies, you are everywhere – I ask you to consider the inner life of the
student who sits, often reluctantly, before you. Your task is to take that
particular person into the living field of your discipline and in some way
to change him by so doing.*

No transformation, no education!

Introduction

Václav Havel once wrote: 'the main instrument of society's self-
knowledge is its culture'.[1] Some teachers might still endorse his
proposition but, of course, it can quickly generate a number of
negative questions. What, for example, if the dominant culture
of any particular society tends to promote self-ignorance or self-
indifference or self-indulgence or some form of self-alienation?
And what if that culture, in one way or another, for whatever
reason, conscious or unconscious, tends to withhold the cultural
means for the continuous development of thinking, feeling and
imagining? What then? What if the educational forces of that
society are essentially disfiguring of human life?

In this opening chapter I want to describe and evoke the inner
dynamics of authentic education, the seminal nature of real
aesthetic and intellectual enquiry. What spiritual values, what
cultural virtues, are embedded in our work as we actively guide
students into the making, performing and evaluating of artistic
work and into the whole culture of the particular art form we
represent? Or when we ask them to engage in the art of thinking
or the complex perspectival hermeneutics of interpretation? What
are the dynamics of the activity released and what kind of image
of the good society do they entail? And how do those dynamics
and how does that image relate to the dominant international mass
culture, the rampant consumer democracy of our times and the
postmodernist thinking which, inevitably, marks our age?

These are most difficult questions. They need to be given a sharp
radical edge and a dissident amplification – even a new reading –
in the present context of our general cultural impoverishment

and the relentless bureaucratic standardization of teachers and teaching.

Alex's fairy story

However, I want to begin this book not with theory, but with a typical example of practice. The modest and rather typical event I will now describe took place recently in my own teaching at the University of Sussex in England but, in principle, it could have taken place in any authentic educational context anywhere in the world. I am not concerned to describe the event in detail, but rather to disclose the educational assumptions that inform it, to delineate the matrix of values and assumptions which make such work possible.

On a Tuesday, then, in the Autumn term three MA students arrive to make short autobiographical presentations in any expressive medium of their choice. One of them is a Russian student, Alex, and she has chosen to make her presentation in the form of a fairy story in what she calls 'the violent tradition of Russian fairy tales'. The group of students sit informally round the table. After a brief introduction, she begins the reading of her story:

> Once upon a time there was a woman neither beautiful nor plain, neither clever, nor stupid, neither kind nor cruel. One day she gave birth to twins. So beautiful were the twins that she loved them more than her own life. The twins opened their eyes, looked upon their mother and cried, and the woman was frightened: what if the children should see the beauty of the world and should find something more wonderful than their mother and will not love her. And she decided: 'Better all my life I shall be their guide than let them love anyone more than me,' and she cut out their eyes.
>
> Some time had passed and the children learned to walk, and in spite of their blindness they began to stray away from their mother. Again she was frightened: what if the children should run too fast and too far for her to keep up with them. And she decided: 'Better all my life I shall carry them on my back than let them abandon me,' and she cut off their legs.
>
> Some more time passed and the children learned to speak, and they began to ask their mother questions about their eyes and legs. Again the woman was frightened: what if the

children should accuse her of cruelty? And she decided: 'Better they never sing a single song than I should hear a word of reproach from them,' and she cut their tongues out . . .²

It is a shocking story; elemental, violent, inexorable. In the story, the mother buries herself and one of her crippled children alive rather than allow him freedom. The second cripple, however, escapes. Hidden away in a valley, he slowly regains the use of his limbs, his eyes and his tongue. Yet, even so, the story ends on a tormenting note of injustice – for the newly restored tongue can only utter a sense of outrage:

And in his despair he remembered his brother with whom he shared his mother's womb and the loneliness of his childhood and he cried; 'Who and why and how and by what right, has deprived me and my brother of the world, of the love and of life itself?'³

The story ends as tragedy, but in the introductory note which Alex read at the beginning she observed:

The life's record is up to date and leaves the tale ending on a very sad and morbid note. The writer may only hope that the future will provide a concluding part to his story in which he might be transformed from a pathetic victim of circumstances into a triumphant hero and might live happily ever after.

What is going on here in this act of art-making and performing? At the level of factual description, it seems simple enough. A fairy story is being told to a group of students who, because of the particular conditions set for the work, are responding to it both as a fairy story and an allegory for the life of the person reading it. Such an event – a presentation of a piece of artwork, complete or nearly complete, to a group of students who, in turn, have just presented or are about to – is an essential part of good arts education. It is the central drama at the heart of the work, often providing the highest moments of absorbed attention and fulfilment. Yet the psychological and symbolic processes involved in these moments are extremely complex, densely interwoven and all but defy adequate formulation. I want to concentrate on the manifold of educational expectations which make it possible, and give it a particular kind of learning dynamic utterly antithetical to that spawned by the ubiquitous 'aims and objectives' sheets which come in advance of the subtle existential engagement of teaching and the degrading evaluation forms which follow in its wake.

I want first to consider the individual presentation of the student and then the context which has elicited it.

In creating the fairy story, Alex has found an artistic form for her own experience. She has found in her own Russian culture a way of transposing what she sees as the essential drama of her life into an allegorical narrative. While the story is compelling in its own right, it carries at the same time the painful burden of her life. It is not her life, of course. It is a representation of it and, therefore, in principle, open to all kinds of editing and re-description. Through working on a popular genre, Alex has made herself an object of her own contemplation. She has created a symbolic world which allows her to shape and reshape, revise and revision, her own hidden and subjective life. She has become a creative agent within the life of culture, a maker of stories and a potential remaker of herself.

The sense of hope accompanying the project is very tangible, not only in Alex's remark, couched in the exact idiom of fairy stories – that she may one day become a triumphant heroine and live happily ever after – but also in the fact (revealed in the discussion after her reading) that she has sent the story to her brother challenging him to continue it. The desire not only for representation but also for a positive and collaborative re-description is obvious. The literal past is always over but the symbolic retelling – and the elaboration of its personal meaning – remains the compelling task of the present and the future, and requires not only memory but also imagination. In this case the genre chosen supports the inner hope – for most fairy stories *do* have happy resolutions. The next chapter remains to be written.

However, the story has been also created for her fellow students who sit and listen. The fairy tale is her formal introduction to the group. This is what she has chosen to bring to it. And here we can locate a crucial element in the transaction. The group – the first most intimate audience to the artwork – are being asked to witness the truth of the art and to recognize its intimate relationship to her actual life. This would seem to involve a second vital distancing and placing. Already an object, standing free from the creator, the art now enters the collective arena. The simple performance – in this case, the reading out of the story – brings the work unequivocally into the collective imagination. This involves acts of cognition and recognition which may well be essential to any further development of the student as well as to the group. Here we are at the very heart of the dynamic which both holds the group together and, simultaneously, generates much of the vital symbolic material for subsequent artistic elaboration and reflection.

So the rhythm of Alex's work has moved from the act of making, to the act of presenting, to the act of witnessing by the group. And all of this not only contributes to the life of consciousness but, more immediately, *is* the life of consciousness as through the sequence of events it seeks ever more form, clarification and integration. I want to suggest that what we have here is a minute, germinating, democratic culture moving, in an uncertain and fluid way, to self-knowledge or possible self-knowledge. The small functional room – Room 302 in EDB – in which the event is happening is, at best, a kind of cultural polis, a communal arena in which the individuals in the group interact to recognize each other, challenge and extend each other's understanding, both of art and life. It could be called a Community of Recognition through the arts and 'creative writing' in this case – but, of course, it could equally as well be through the Humanities or the Sciences.

However, the work is not coming out of the blue. It is not a 'happening'. It is not a chance event. It is not a natural eruption from the unconscious; it is more like a ritual and a spiritual drama. The presentation has been invited as part of an educational programme grounded on a number of principles. These principles may never be fully formulated in the actual work – they may lie tacit and work at the level of guiding assumptions – yet they remain axiomatic to it. They form a paradigm at the base of what we do. I would like to outline three of the key principles which, seen in reciprocal interaction, may further illuminate the encompassing context in which Alex is working and take us closer to the inner dynamic of authentic education.

The three reciprocal principles of educational activity

Education is existential in nature

That is the first principle. Put in a negative form, it means that education cannot take place against the intentions of the student or without his or her active participation. It is true that existence has become an unfashionable category, but it remains a primary one. The word existential derives from the Latin *existere* and means literally *to stand out*. Its original sense of *standing out* developed through the idea of *emerging* and *being visible* to that of *existing*. The verb indicates that as individuals we have to step out of the background of our lives into the foreground, that the mere fact of being alive is nothing. To exist is to make ourselves visible, to declare ourselves, to confess ourselves, to become the free and willing agents of our own actions and understanding. Just as no one can be ethically good for us or aesthetically experience for us, so no one can educationally learn for us. Learning may be released by a teacher but it can never be conferred – for it is not an object so much as a particular cast of mind, a creative and critical orientation towards experience. The student has to learn to become the protagonist of his or her own learning. This means that in the teaching of any intellectual or artistic discipline there must be open structures – gaps for the unknown, gaps for reflection, gaps for revision, gaps for contemplation, gaps for questions, gaps for the imagination, gaps for the Socratic elenchus,[4] gaps which constantly invite, provoke, unsettle and support the deep self-involvement of the student.

For this reason in my own teaching I always ask students who they are and what they wish to learn. I often invite the students to begin with autobiographical work – with the drama and the narrative of the self, with the fairy story by Alex. I begin with the individual having to stand out, having to shape something personal about themselves which cannot be taken out of the textbooks nor relayed by anyone else in the group. If, as the novelist Milan Kundera has remarked, existence is being perpetually overlooked, then it is for the teacher to bring it back and make it the fine inner core of activity again.

According to the first principle, the teacher is a releaser, a midwife, aiming to give birth to existential acts of learning and spiritual engagement in the student. The purpose is not to prescribe settled narratives of meaning, but to engender a quest in search of what is not yet known, of what may never be known, of what is emotionally alluring but somehow badly out of focus. To this extent, it could be called a postmodern pedagogy, but it is also classical in its origins.

Education is essentially a collaborative activity

This is the second principle; and it brings us at once to an obvious paradox. The individual who is to develop needs a community. In fact, the individual is inconceivable without the notion of others and of relationship with others. If the I exists it is because the we exists, or in the rather more eloquent Swahili version: *I am because we are.* In western culture the educational implications of this truth were first elaborated by Socrates and recorded in the philosophical plays of his student, Plato. For Socrates, the existential act of enquiry arises not in cultivated isolation, but in animated dialogue, in the disciplined narrative of conversation, in the careful exploration of opposed conceptions as uttered by various individuals engaged in the common pursuit of understanding. Learning becomes a philosophical drama between people who do not necessarily agree, but who wish to find out. Indeed, Socrates claimed that he could only think effectively when there was someone there offering a counter view. Without a conversation to participate in, without the shock of difference, he regarded himself as intellectually sterile, a philosopher without an idea in his head. In the Socratic method the notion of truth is often confined to the logical development of concepts – this is one of its major critical limitations – but the principle of learning being an open spirited engagement not *in* but *between* people is seminal and lies at the very foundation of western culture, being one of its most subversive and, at the moment, most threatened elements.

Such collaboration depends on trust that the collective pursuit is committed to the unknown outcome of the intellectual or artistic activity – concerned, that is to say, not with what is clearly partisan or narrowly ideological, but with the specific truth of what appears to be emerging in the creation of *this* argument or *this* particular piece of artwork or the contemplation of *this* fairy story, as it is being read by this student to this group, as it is happening between us *now*. The teacher must struggle to ensure that the activity is open, at least in principle, to all relevant perspectives, is always open to revision and is expressive of all those seriously engaged in it. This educational process is the very antithesis of a private activity: it is also impossible to quantify and measure though its mesmerising power is palpable and observed, by any sensitive onlooker, in a flash. In the case of Socrates even his death – his death, most of all – provided both an existential opportunity and an absolute inner drama for collaborative enquiry.

The second principle, then, establishes the teacher as coordinator, conductor and democrat.

Education is always a cultural activity which has to be continuously deepened and extended

This is the third principle. It calls for a progressive initiation of the student into the culture of the discipline which extends and deepens the existential and collaborative process. The richer the cultural material, the greater the possible development. If, as Roger Scruton has argued, 'the immediacy of subjective awareness is an index of its emptiness'[5] then to depend entirely on what has been existentially proffered or collaboratively worked on could easily result in an unremitting superficiality.

What has to be grasped is the intimate connection between symbol and consciousness. The more extensive and subtle the symbolism the greater the possibilities for the articulate flowering of consciousness. According to this third principle education exists to set up a conversation down the ages and across the cultures, across both time and space, so that students are challenged by other ways of understanding and, at the same time, acquire ever new materials – metaphors, models, ideas, images, narratives, facts – for shaping and reshaping and testing again that never finished process, their own intellectual and spiritual lives. The third principle calls for endless acts of cultural reincarnation – acts which enable students to see with new eyes and to speak with new tongues. This extends the growing collaboration between the group to the whole of historic culture and brings the existential quest into relationship with all other such quests down the ages. Alex's work, because it has chosen the genre of the fairy tale, already operates inside the field of all other fairy stories. It is already, because of its chosen genre, inside a cultural tradition. The value of these traditions will be examined in some depth in relation to autobiography in Chapter 5. The task of teaching is to make the connections, to move backwards and forwards across time to weave the cultural cloth. Without this third principle, arts education could easily become a kind of freewheeling Californian encounter group, limited to its own resources and its immediate assumptions and without any alternative wisdom or perspectives to draw on – and yet blissfully ignorant of its radical impoverishment. The alterity of historic culture is also essential because no individual can possess the wholeness of truth, always an ideal construction and a deceptive intellectual projection, or fully encompass the many ways of interpreting the multiform character of life. In this sense, historic culture, in a technological age often ignorantly disparaged, can act as both a disconcerting and chastening energy.

Our third principle casts the teacher in the role of cultural guardian and initiator into the symbolic life, as connector and water diviner.

The three principles acting together create the authentic field of educational activity. This activity was eloquently captured by John Dewey when he declared: 'education must be conceived as a continuing reconstruction of experience: that the process and the goal are one and the same thing'.[6] It is these principles which, though largely unformulated in the immediate work, have invisibly shaped the context in which Alex presents her work to the group for response and recognition and, even, revision.

What, then, are the values of the activity? They are the politics of the educational process itself. The group regulates itself in a public space. It comes to its conclusions through the tangible presentation of art and the working through of arguments relating to its fitting interpretation. It makes its decisions openly and freely. The work involves acts of making, witnessing, and evaluating; it involves a dialectic of asking questions and examining answers. It also includes an engagement with some of the many 'answers' given in the cultural inheritance – whether in the form of art or theory or spiritual example. And whatever is discovered remains always provisional, always open, at least in principle, to further experimentation or argument or contemplation. For each student it is a vulnerable reaching out within the encompassing trust of the fellow community of learners.

Education, art and postmodernism

The Community of Recognition is, as a model, a tiny cultural democracy dedicated to art and enquiry. It is built on freedom, on personal engagement, on social collaboration, on cultural connection and the deep desire for transpersonal recognition. I would like to suggest that this is the spiritual dynamic of authentic education and the social values intrinsic to its modus operandi. But what is the relationship of these to the mass culture 'outside', to the dominant political reality and to the various claims made by the postmodernists? Is it possible to ground our educational activity in the wider social domain?

The prevailing democracy, in contrast to our Community of Recognition, would seem to be a rather abstract and over-centralized affair; its political life, except at the time of elections, is distant from the individual and most of its art seems to be slickly prefabricated in advance, requiring little personal response or recognition for its fulfilment. Most of mass culture is manufactured to satisfy commercial ends and is as far removed from self-knowledge as an amusement arcade is from teaching philosophy. In the form of advertising much of it exists to indoctrinate while in the form of art much of it exists to anaesthetize, to arrest that active movement from diffuse self-consciousness to articulate self-awareness which is one of the principal aims of education to engender. It is characteristic of television and video channels to be structured as seamless flows, endless streams of self-cancellation, with never a moment's gap to invite reflection or evaluation. Their very mode of presentation banishes the Socratic elenchus. Thus an ever-dissolving sequence of images is hooked into a system of pre-critical sensations; whatever enters the visual flow is immediately deprived of significance. As postmodernists have rightly observed, this has led to a state where there is no meaning – only simulacra, without sense, without history. Jean Baudrilland, with some characteristic hyberbole, describes the cultural predicament when he writes:

> Every set of phenomena . . . has to be fragmented, disjointed, so that it can be sent down the circuits; every kind of language has to be resolved into a binary formulation so that it can circulate not, any longer, in our memories, but in the luminous, electronic memory of the computers. No human language can withstand the speed of light. No event can withstand being beamed across the whole planet. No history can withstand the centrifugation of facts or their being short-circuited in real time . . .[7]

The problem with most postmodernists like Baudrillard is that they show us no way beyond this unprecedented crisis in representation. In the end, many of them seem to become the celebrants of the invasive electronic glossolalia rather than its discriminating critics.

Most self-confessed postmodernists would seem to celebrate a freewheeling electronic cultural eclecticism or, at least, tolerate it with an ironic smile. The world's a carnival of changing images, sound bites and endless quotations; it is a glossy supermarket of vying lifestyles. Such a hyperreality is regarded as the inevitable outcome of an advanced electronic age of communications: of the computer, of the word-processor, Internet, of television and video, where information floats free of its historic and existential context and where art is presented as entertainment, often inseparable from advertising and general hype and where the two modes – of fact and fiction – all but coexist. For the postmodernists all culture becomes a matter of style, display, appearance, rhetoric. Indeed, donning a glittering coat of irony some of them are quick to convert their own thinking into fashion and all of them would seem to espouse the relativitism and eclecticism that informs the dominant consumer culture. They seem unable to point to oppositional energies or to excavate the buried sources of transcendence. They are like glittering water spiders riding the turbid waters.

In brief, the problem is that postmodernist thinking tends to lock us even further into a mass culture that we need to be critical of. In essentially endorsing the status quo it deprives us of other ways of conceiving, imagining and desiring. If all cultural expressions are equal, if all differences are to be merged, if all classifications are to be declassified, then we are robbed of a sense of significance and deprived, at once, of any real concept of education (such as defined earlier in my three axioms). For if all things are utterly relative, there can be no leading out, no advance, no imaginative or intellectual accumulation. If *all* things are absolutely relative, nothing matters; and if nothing matters, the public space is quickly colonized by the most ruthless and the most rapacious, the thug and the quack. In as much as postmodernism marks the end of a certain kind of modernism and the beginning of a sympathetic reconnection with the whole of historic culture and a certain subtle perspectivalism – a contemporary version of the Socratic elenchus – it is to be welcomed; but in as much as it marks an uncritical acceptance of mindless consumerism and a denial of all trans-personal value and meaning it has to be severely questioned.

Nearly twenty years ago Neil Postman, in his brilliant study *Amusing Ourselves To Death*, took the city of Las Vegas as the icon of today's international culture, glossily alive with an endless stream of manipulated desire. What Postman saw emerging, through the shaping power of television and the electronic media, was a culture in which all public discourse had become a mode of entertainment, where all symbolic life was a variant of show business. 'Cosmetics', he wrote laconically, 'has replaced ideology'; and went on to point out that 'censorship is not a necessity when all political life takes the form of a jest'.[8] The evidence of such a society is all around us. We have only to open our eyes to begin to chronicle it.

Most of mass culture is a surrogate culture. It robs its citizens of the materials they most need for the fulfilment of their freedom. It also tends to rob them of all the other cultural visions they need to keep their reflection bright and their minds expansive. In his Foreword to *Brave New World*, Aldous Huxley wrote:

> A really efficient totalitarian state would be one in which the all-powerful executive of political bosses and their army of managers control a population of slaves who do not have to be coerced, because they love their servitude.[9]

Such a totalitarian society would not feel like one, of course. It would, even, parade its freedom and its happiness, especially in its tabloid 'newspapers'.

Yet, at the same time, it would seem equally clear that the dominant democratic society *does* allow for freedom of thought and argument and *does* protect many individual rights. The strength of these legally encoded rights is that they protect the individual from abuse; but their weakness is that they invariably operate outside a positive conception of the good society. In their formulation they do not affirm the social and cultural conditions within which individual rights can be best realized. During the last two decades an international culture driven by vast technological and economic powers, which is dedicated almost exclusively to the making of profits and the frenetic buying and selling of goods and services, has emerged. While the 'pursuit of happiness' has become a private matter, the public spaces have become colonized by market forces. That space for the transpersonal – that arena where the personal and collective meet to animate each other – has closed in and virtually disappeared. In the emerging consumer-civilization the old public spaces have been ravaged by market forces and are desperately occupied by the new dispossessed, and the private spaces, especially where they are opulent, are defended with iron spikes, grids, alarm systems, barking Alsatians and rented guards. We find not the drama of collaboration, but the drama of division; not a common community but a society driven by subcultures and carved up divisively by market managers into commercial niches; not schools or universities working together but institutions at war with each other in the frenetic competition for material advantage. (This, as I implied earlier, is the economic background for many of the cultural insights provided by the postmodernists).

In such a civilization the appeal to democratic values, while not exactly false, becomes deeply unconvincing. The liberal rhetoric fails to match the collective reality. It is as if from under the proclamation of human rights – partly articulated in the eighteenth century by educated gentlemen with the Greek polis in mind – there has grown a smooth overarching managerial culture disseminated by global organizations, with a dramatically different set of symbols, values, relationships and expectations. This system does not deny the traditional democratic rights deriving from the Enlightenment, but under and over them spins a different kind of culture, based on leisure, consumption, services, lifestyle, display, appearance and the endless, ruthless competition for markets. In the new global consumer society, there is a danger that freedom becomes largely confined to a choice between supermarkets, items and brand names; that happiness becomes reformulated as the need for fun (and the display of style) and the citizen (and student) is recast as consumer or customer.

Against the current erosions of meaning and value we can begin to see more clearly the seminal value of the politics and dynamics of authentic teaching. The Community of Recognition provide a truer sense of democracy and a richer sense of participatory culture, a culture closer to the primary processes of making, presenting and evaluating – directed by the need for exploration and social confirmation. Teaching of this kind offers not only a living democratic model but also a vivid apprenticeship into the making and sharing of embodied meanings (however provisional) and the making and sharing of collaborative relationships. Further-more, it is not difficult to root this practice in a long tradition of thinking which has been concerned to place freedom within the embodied life of culture and community. This tradition has been represented by such educationists as Josiah Royce, John Dewey and Maxine Greene and by such thinkers as Hannah Arendt,

Jürgen Habermas and Charles Taylor. It has one of its major sources in the philosophical writings of Hegel. For in Hegel's philosophy a primary significance is given to the place of recognition in the continuous making of culture. In the Hegelian myth the Slave discovers his repressed humanity and triumphs over his hedonistic Master through labour and the art of making, which releases the power of reflection and a growing sense of spiritual autonomy. Not only is there a right to private property and the free expression of opinion in Hegel, but these rights are placed in a broader culture which seeks its own fullest realization. At the base there is the freedom for the market, but at the apex there is the freedom for the collaborative pursuit of meaning and the articulation of the spirit. It is the latter qualitative freedom (embodied in the life of a real culture, within a public space) that is so absent in post-modernist thinking and in our consumer society at large. One of the spiritual functions of the Community of Recognition should be to represent and reanimate it. It was once conceived as the very acme of education – but no longer. In the study of English, students now compose advertisements; in media studies they describe the themes of the TV soaps; in art design they invent further glossy packages for shampoo and beefburgers. And, before very long, it is likely that the multinationals will be running the educational 'business' to secure an even greater fix between talent and the market economy.

In *Between Past and Future* Hannah Arendt (1961) offered this description of politics:

> If, then, we understand the political in the sense of the polis, its end or *raison d'être* would be to establish and keep in existence a space where freedom as virtuosity can appear. This is the realm where freedom is a worldly reality, tangible in words which can be heard, in deeds which can be seen, and in events which are talked about, remembered, and turned into stories before they are finally incorporated into the great storybook of human history. Whatever occurs in this space of appearances is political by definition, even when it is not a direct product of action.[10]

I want to suggest that Hannah Arendt's formulation illuminates both the democratic nature of the good society and also acts as an eloquent description of the Community of Recognition. There is, then, a broader political tradition in which the model of authentic learning can be grounded and, if my brief description of today's society is at all accurate, its political value and cultural role must be only too clear.

Conclusion

At times in this chapter I have assumed that the dynamic educational model is still possible in our state educational system; but it could well be that this is less and less the case. Education in its dominant institutional form has become training, has become investment, has become business and management, has become delivery of skills, has become measuring and grading and ranking, has become social control and certification – but it has *not* become an initiation of individuals into the art of authentic learning, into the resonant Community of Recognition. In a recent incident concerning a headmaster in England taking a long holiday in term-time, the school's chairman was reported to have said: 'We are running a £6 million business. We regard the head as our chief executive. The governors . . . have made a business decision and I am flabbergasted that people are critical'.[11] The model in action here is explicit enough.

Adapting to the pressures of their immediate society teachers themselves have become alienated from the profound Community of Recognition and are often – unwittingly or unwillingly – the active agents of alienation, cultural dispossession and the general intellectual dumbing down. They have become the compliant civil servants of the status quo, rather than authentic educators, ironically closer to the standardising imperatives of the global multinationals than to the subtle individuating imperatives of the educational pursuit engendered by Socrates. If this is true, it is impossible to quantify the loss or begin to articulate its long-term consequences for the human spirit.

After writing and presenting her story about her own life with its suppression of freedom, Alex had declared: 'The writer may only hope that the future will provide a concluding part to his story in which he might be transformed from a pathetic victim of circumstances into a triumphant hero and might live happily ever after.' Such a hope and such a desire for freedom must also provide the political and spiritual energy for the renewal of authentic teaching. This calls for nothing less than a revolution in both current thinking and practice. The chances are it will not happen; but it is also true that the power of the spirit works in startling ways and what is repressed now, constellating in the unconscious, can suddenly be released and transform what, until that unpredicted historic moment, looked like the inevitable and unchanging state of things. This has been the story of western culture. So there is some reason for hope. Moreover, within the Community of Recognition itself, nothing can quite expunge the transcendental moments of educational advance and inner enlightenment.

Chapter 2

On the spiritual in art, culture and education

All seeing is from a perspective. All interpretation is precisely that, interpretation: one way of judging, of making tentative sense, of seeking a coherence which yet remains, forever, unstable, shifting, inconstant. This chapter is written by a man who was brought up as a Christian on the Norfolk coast of England in the post-war years. My grandparents on my father's side were Methodists: on my mother's side they were Roman Catholics. It was never a happy union of faiths. They almost never met. My father's parents were determined never to set foot inside any church which smelt of incense and which housed idolatrous statues of the Virgin Mary. My mother's parents, on the other hand, knew with an infallible assurance they had a divinely sanctioned route to the true God and didn't have to bother with any counter claims made by upstart Methodists.

As a boy under my mother's influence I progressively identified with Catholicism until I decided, with some Machiavellian nudging by the parish priest, that I had a vocation. I wanted to be a Franciscan but ended up in a seminary for missionary priests – Mill Hill Fathers they were called. I was twelve. I lasted the regime for two or more years and then left and from that time, slowly, year by year, the hold of my faith lessened. I struggled through my adolescence with the growing hole left by the disappearance of God. I felt the need for a world illuminated by values but experienced often a desolate emptiness within and a mordant awareness of mortality.

In brief, I had lost my childhood faith but remained preoccupied with the spiritual dimension. Life, I instinctively felt, had to be about more than could be grasped through the blind operations of chance and the indifferent engines of insentient matter. I also felt, perhaps rather diffusely, that any concept of education worthy of the name had to engage with the perennial issues relating to freedom, to meaning, to value – however broken the world seemed. Indeed, the more the world was broken apart the more it demanded from us a counter philosophical and symbolic activity. We had to connect even if it was a matter of logging differences, divisions, distinctions.

This chapter, at one level, is a rather personal affair. What is written comes out of a particular culture, a particular time, a particular set of preoccupations, a particular person. And yet, at another level, there is an argument here which requires general attention. So much of our contemporary culture seems devoid of animating spirit and the art of human cherishing. So many of our schools resemble functional offices without character, charisma or charm. The former, surely, relates to the ubiquitous commodification of life; the latter to its obsessive certification.

It is as if, ironically, in the consumer West we have won the ideological war but, at the very same moment, lost the poetic spirit, the solidarity of communion, the zest of life. If these words seem somewhat vague then in this chapter I will try to make them precise. Certainly, if we are to address the ethically vacuous state of consumer society and the increasingly functional character of our educational system, we have no choice but to raise seminal questions and in the dominant Zeitgeist of relativity and protective irony, we must do so with as much courage as we can dare. In such a spirit these words have been written – but, in the nature of things, they can be no more than fragmentary notes, jottings put in an empty bottle and hurled out to sea.

Introduction

From time to time one can be haunted by a paralysing dread: that we are stranded at the beginning of a new millennium in a culture where all spiritual resources have been spent, where shopping is the last world religion, where the latest Tesco is the last cathedral and where the concept of consumerism is the last idea. It is as if one had dreamt of the vast ocean or high paths over the Alps and woken to find onself confined to a shopping arcade for the rest of one's life, as if one had dreamt of a vision of irresistible beauty and then been compelled to watch a trite simulation of what one had seen, linked to some international brand name, staring back from the video screen. It is as if nothing further remains but the electronic regurgitation of clichés and with it, as its inevitable consequence, the permanent wiping out of sensitive and discriminating consciousness. The fear is that schools, colleges and universities have become no more than corporations run by managers for the collective standardization of life and that the multinationals, like McDonald's, are patiently waiting in the wings to colonize them so as to secure their convergent innocent customers for the life of eternal consumption.

At the beginning of the twenty-first century this would seem to be our own peculiar version of hell – a life utterly banal, seemingly happy, becoming increasingly global, yet devoid of all ethical or metaphysical purpose. For thousands of years nothing but the TV smile, the fatuous jingle, designer clothes and the apparent servicing of the consumer's every want. The end of history – with the plausible lie left on continuous replay. On bad days we seem close to inhabiting such an anodyne dystopia. On better days we struggle to tear off the tacky film which covers our educational and poetic aspirations, resist the counterfeit version of consciousness and struggle to locate the smothered springs of renewal.

In this chapter I want to define and evoke the nature of the spiritual in relationship to our postmodern consumer age. It is somewhat ironic, given the mechanistic nature of the National Curriculum, that even government missives can insist on the spiritual and aesthetic dimension. A recent circular entitled 'Religious Education and Collective Worship', for example, claimed:

> The government is concerned that insufficient attention has been paid explicitly to the spiritual, moral and cultural aspects of pupils' development and would encourage schools to address how the curriculum and other activities might best contribute to this crucial dimension of education.[1]

I will address this seminal, if uncomfortable, theme with the seriousness it deserves, with the seriousness the government has never seriously given it. I will attempt to break through the pious rhetoric of government edicts to locate the precarious state of the human spirit and its palpable absence in much of our culture.

My concern is, particularly, related to the making of the arts both in the wider society as well as in our schools, colleges, and universities. Such a task requires a re-evaluation of the word 'spiritual', a recognition of the demise of orthodox Christianity as also a greater understanding of the way in which true art creates a living mythology of consciousness. Although many are now turning to science and technology for their interpretation of human life, it yet remains the specific burden of authentic art to illuminate the elusive nature of our ephemeral lives – or so I shall argue.

Broadening our understanding of the spiritual

In our consumer culture spirituality has become a problematical concept. The words traditionally used to describe our sense of ultimate value – words such as *sacred, holy, spiritual, divine, sublime* – have become the language of deep hesitancy and embarrassment, the half-displaced concepts of perpetual unease. They have no secure place in a highly technological society, nor do they belong to the consumer society with its free-market economy, nor to the prevailing postmodern sensibility where the coolness of irony and relativity prevail. They are uncomfortable words, haunted words, ambivalent words; they remind us, simultaneously, of redemptive possibilities which we feel we have permanently forfeited and of supernatural positions we regard as intellectually discredited. The words seem to side with a world of Upper Case Letters and Grand Narratives that in our age of postmodernism and global awareness we feel we can no longer embrace with conviction or integrity.

For most people in the West the word spirituality is still formally linked to Christianity and to at least some working acceptance of its major tenets. Historically, this makes compelling sense. Christianity has been for centuries, at least in Europe, the dominant matrix for the spiritual development of the individual. Many of the greatest symbolic achievements of our culture, especially in the arts, are unthinkable without it and this remains true right down to the present moment. Yet it would seem an elementary category mistake to define spirituality in exclusively Christian terms. One can envisage a deep spirituality entirely free from Christian belief or even antithetical to it. Such a spirituality could, of course, be based on another of the world religions – but, more importantly, it could be based entirely on itself. For spirituality is an intrinsic part of human existence – it can be experienced in particular moments of relationship, of erotic love, of heightened perception, and of high creativity; in states of trance, self-transcendence and spontaneous enthusiasm, as in those unexpected moments of timelessness when the sheer inexpungable strangeness of consciousness quietly reveals itself.

The spiritual dimension can, also, be located in moments of acute personal crisis and near-breakdown: in moments of abandonment and anxiety – in the dark shadows of life on the other side of the 'happy' consumer society. These states of inner disruption and inner dislocation – of unease and disease – invariably release the subverting metaphysical question: *What for? What ultimately for?* Such experiences of the spiritual – or the acute and desolating sense of its absence – do not depend on any prior religious creed. They arise from our predicament as reflective beings as they also point to our often unclaimed and untapped potentiality. Adapting one of the formulations of Yeats, one could say that the spiritual is a crisis that joins the buried self for certain moments to the trivial daily mind. These illuminating and terrifying moments of experience precede theology as they also transcend it. It is the very nature of the spirit that it goes beyond the concept and can be gloriously ineffable, as it can also be hauntingly dark.

We need, in truth, to broaden the notion of the spiritual, to release it from many of its historic Christian associations and to reconceive it as a definitive element of human nature and human potentiality, an abiding expression of our predicament and our creative response to it. Perhaps against all the relativizing tendencies of the postmodern sensibility we need, tentatively, to conceive it as a universal element within human experience. We are spiritual animals, half in nature, half out of nature, in quest of understanding, vital connection and recognition. The spiritual element in us seeks an affirmative relationship to our predicament, a sense of wholeness and belonging, literally an *at-one-ment* – though this, as I shall suggest later, has become a deeply problematic part of its nature. The arts, when they are significant, are invariably engaged with these perennial matters – with the question of human meaning and human transformation, with the kinds of redemption and forms of affirmation which may be open to us, as well as with the natural limitations that may thwart and even destroy our highest aspirations. The crucifixion is, after all, one of the archetypes of the spiritual narrative and central to the iconography of western culture, as tragedy is one of its earliest dramatic genres.

The spiritual function of Romantic and modern art

With the gradual decline of Christianity, the arts progressively took on an urgent spiritual significance. As early as 1757 Swedenborg declared that the churches had ceased to be vehicles of the spiritual life, claiming that they were destined to remain little more than empty shells. The extravagant and often vulgar displays of the Baroque illustrate only too vividly a religion which had become a mixture of propaganda and hype, a kind of cloying kitsch, its bombastic rhetoric extravagantly masking the growing unease of the Christian churches. During the slow period of religious dissolution the art-maker was often to step into the role of the priest and in a time of increasing disenchantment keep the need for metaphysical meaning and human fulfilment on the agenda. William Blake wrote around the year 1820 that: 'Jesus and his apostles and Disciples were all Artists'[2] and that 'A Poet, a Painter, a Musician, an Architect: the Man or Woman who is not one of these is not a Christian'[3] and continued with the following rhapsodic utterances:

> You must leave Fathers and Mothers and Houses and Lands if they stand in the way of art. Prayer is the study of Art. Praise is the Practice of Art. Fasting etc all relate to Art. The outward ceremony is Antichrist. The Eternal Body of Man is The Imagination, that is God himself.[4]

God defined as the Imagination. Here we can locate a remarkable transposition of Christian doctrine from the supernatural to the poetic – as also in Blake's radical definition of the Bible as 'the Great Code of Art.'[5] About six years later Blake's ardent young disciple painted himself resembling Christ, a clear halo circling his head, staring triumphantly out: Saint Samuel Palmer, artist, committed to the holy powers of the Imagination (see Plate 1).

Through the nineteenth century the arts often took on that broad spiritual function so strikingly announced by Blake and Palmer. The aesthetic became akin to the sacramental; and the artist became priest and hierophant or, more often, the unwanted shaman, the creative outsider, the disturbing prophet. And what was to be revealed in so many works of art was visionary perception freed from the constricting cages of doctrine and the dark, airless cells of institutional dogma – the quick of living apprehension and not the dry dust of inherited propositions. In so much Romantic and modern art the divine became compellingly immanent, the sacred was brought back to earth, the holy made intimate, the projections of the divine reclaimed as transcendent aspects of our humanity. Van Gogh in one of his many letters to his brother talked of a new religion: 'which will have no name, but which will have the same effect of consoling, of making life possible, which the Christian religion used to have'[6] and talked about the use of radiant, vibrating colours to represent 'something of the eternal which the halo used to symbolize'.[7] In the early twentieth century Kandinsky was to address colour in a similar way – as a grammar of the metaphysical – as he was also to define the arts as the 'mightiest agencies' of spiritual life.[8] Later still Rothko, in search of the sublime, was to take it to its most abstract intensity in his own work and demand a sacred building for its display.

Indeed, we stand in need of an alternative, subverting history of modernism, a history which would bring out, against all the dominant formalist and historicist interpretations, the striking concern, at least among most of its seminal proponents, with the sacred, the archetypal and the mythical.[9] This concern continued right through the twentieth century among many of the greatest artists, whatever the dominant fashion or journalist tag, and provided one essential continuity with the Romantic movement. Such a history would accord a certain primacy to the declared aesthetic and spiritual intentions of the artists themselves. Consider, for example, the way in which the artist Max Beckmann (see Plate 2) envisaged the artist's task in his *Self-portrait with a Glass Ball* (1956). As an art-maker, Beckmann holds rather protectively the round green mandala which it is his burden and privilege both to make and to bear. His alchemical work makes what is broken whole and what is ordinary magical. In a lecture given in 1938 Max Beckmann was to declare:

> Art is creative for the sake of realisation, not for amusement; for transfiguration, not for the sake of play. It is the quest of our self that drives us along a never ending journey we must all make.[10]

This is the unadorned language of spiritual quest yet it represents the aspiration of some of the greatest artists down to our own postmodern period, even if now all but entirely eclipsed by various movements such as conceptualism and minimalism. That story, which we will pick up again in Chapter 8, has yet to be fully told. Quite simply, the conventional critical maps we have been given barely fit the terrain; for the dominant categories, deriving from either formalism or ideology, are far too crude to catch the spiritual essences. The historic point is that as Christianity has declined, so the gifted art-maker has often stepped in to keep the spiritual questions open and labile.

The fallacy of scientism

Part of the general difficulty in discussing the spiritual is due to a powerful, pervasive, yet quite erroneous assumption that fundamentally our world can be explained through science or through the methods of science, through, that is to say, the systematic elaboration of material causes. The dramatic development of science had, of course, a devastating effect on the credibility of orthodox Christianity. In the seventeenth century, under the systematic observation of the astronomers, it became clear that the earth was very far from being the centre of God's Creation, while in the nineteenth century it became equally clear that humankind had not been uniquely created by God, but had evolved through a turbulent process of natural, selective adaptation. These profound revolutions in understanding exposed many of the cardinal tenets of the Christian faith as hopelessly misconceived. They literally decentred us. At the same time, the practical and ideological triumph of science tended to promote a further kind of fallacy: the view that science was the unique and exclusive means for understanding the true nature of all things; that there was one key to understanding the human world and that it lay with the empirical analysis of matter and the law of causation. Thus the tide of materialism came steadily in; its waves continuously eroding the resonance and referentiality of spiritual language.

In Matthew Arnold's *Dover Beach*, written only eight years after the publication of Darwin's *On The Origin of Species by Natural Selection* (1859), a sense of urgent subjective love is put against an objective world which has become increasingly violent and futile. In *Dover Beach* man becomes the unhoused one, the orphan in an indifferent universe:

> *Ah, love, let us be true*
> *To one another! for the world which seems*
> *To lie before us like a land of dreams,*
> *So various, so beautiful, so new,*
> *Hath really neither joy, nor love, nor light,*

Nor certitude, nor peace, nor help for pain;
And we are here as on a darkling plain
Swept with confused alarms of struggle and flight,
Where ignorant armies clash by night.[11]

Yet it would seem obvious that, whatever the objective universe might be like, we actually inhabit a human world of meanings and intentions – 'Ah, love, let us be true to one another!' – which simply cannot be grasped through an analysis of material causation. For example, no analysis of facial muscles and their operations could ever disclose the meaning of a smile. No analysis of brain tissue could ever disclose the quintessential nature of a living thought or of the import of an ethical category such as justice, hope or goodness. The smile, as with the thought or moral category, can only be understood through human recognition. Any expression of consciousness requires a comparable act of consciousness for its understanding.

Here, without doubt, the deconstructing and relativizing elements of postmodernists have had an important part to play in pulling down the grand narratives and metaphysical pretensions of science with its totalitarian tendency to assume it could interpret every kind of problem. This aspect of postmodern thinking has been a liberation of the mind.

The questions which most needle and haunt us are questions about meaning and meaninglessness, about purpose and futility. These questions can never be adequately answered by abstract and abstracting science, for they derive from our entangled historic, cultural and personal experience and can only be comprehended within that subtle manifold. They can only be properly explored at the level of consciousness and culture from which they emanate. The higher cannot be grasped through the lower. The pattern of atoms and molecules cannot reveal the pattern of consciousness. Any interpretation of human life that is incapable of including the sublime achievement of *The Magic Flute* is drastically incomplete.

Here it is possible that we could gain from a poetic revisioning of the notion of levels of being moving from a vertical base upwards towards the act of human contemplation and comprehension: from the mineral world to the plant, from the plant to the animal, from the animal to that of the reflective and expressive human being. The vertical movement from level to level involves a continuity in the organization of matter and profound discontinuity at the level of being and value. At the apex of the triangle – one evoked by Kandinsky in his *Concerning the Spiritual in Art* – the power of consciousness, by recoiling upon itself as well as by mediating its hidden life through the creation of expressive symbolism, creates the possibility of meaning and freedom, of dilemma and doubt, of fragmentation and reparation. It opens the world to the transformative powers of the imagination and the free play of the creative act. This is not a dualist view, nor is it, in any way, dependent on supernatural conceptions; it is more an ecological way of looking. In a quite fundamental way, spirituality can be conceived as part of, as an unplanned outcome of, the natural world, yet opening up within nature new dimensions of reflection, prophecy and possibility.

It is this distinctive power of consciousness attending to consciousness through sustained acts of recognition and affirmation which illuminates the true nature of spirituality. It is the spiritual in us which aspires towards wholeness, seeks connection, pattern, circumference and desires to live in animated relationship to its discoveries. From this perspective, God could be understood, at the very least, as an imaginative necessity, perhaps the ultimate expression of the human need for transcendence; the three lettered sign denoting alterity.

Towards a contemporary spirituality

The suspended, open, precarious nature of spirituality stands in need of a much more complex recognition. For centuries spirituality appeared to be safely housed in an objective world. In the Classical world the cosmos *meant* order; in the Hebraic world the Creation implied a divine creator. When the precise observations and theoretical deductions of science unhoused Christian believers there was an inevitable crisis in orthodox faith that threatened, for a time, the very idea of spirituality. Yet this traumatic recognition of abandonment, of not necessarily belonging to any grand system of design, to any preordained narrative either in nature or history, of feeling ourselves spiritual orphans in a seemingly indifferent universe – all deeply in tune with the philosophy of postmodernism – served finally to clarify the autonomy of the spiritual. As Carl Jung realized, the plenitude of figures liberally cast upon the face of the universe had to be drawn back and returned to their source in the creative unconscious. The symbolic images had to be given back to the one who symbolized and the gods returned to the ineffable depths of the human mind. For the spiritual does not reside in objects, but in subjects; not in the things of the world but in the unhoused reflective beings who are suspended like dark fertile spiders from that world. Deep subjectivity bears its own spiritual truth; there need be no objective correspondence, no guarantor 'out there', no certainty of any grand narrative or final prescriptive code. Ultimately, from now on, all spirituality has to be radically unhoused. Tellingly, the word *spiritual* derives from the Indo-European word *speis* meaning *a blowing out of breath*. It is as necessary as that, as dynamic as that and as elusive as that. The word religion, in contrast, derives from the Latin *re-ligere* meaning to bind together; but the paradox is that the breath cannot be bound. It is an incoherent metaphor and, if it suggests any image, it is that of suffocation. Systems that would seek to hold the spirit are all but bound to destroy it. That is the depressing story of nearly all world religions. At the beginning of the twenty-first century we are in a unique position to grasp this great, if uncomfortable, truth. Indeed, it could be called a postmodern truth where the postmodern is seen as an incredulity towards all meta-narratives and all systems of final explanation. It denotes a human predicament and a profound orientation of being within that predicament.

The fact that the spiritual cannot be explained by the narratives of history or the teleology of nature or any other grand narrative of theoretical explanation does not mean that it does not exist, nor that it is insignificant. It merely calls for an unsentimental spirituality, a trembling inwardness, liberated from all those congealed dogmas of the historical world-religions, as also from the bogus scientism and gross materialism of the dominant consumer society. When Van Gogh painted himself in 1888 as a Buddhist monk (see Plate 3) he painted an image of a direct, burning spirituality which had freed itself from the theological doctrines of the Christian Church. The man who stares at us from the painting has the courage to confront the world with an ultimate simplicity and beauty of being. This can be seen in the vulnerable face but is also aesthetically embodied in the vibrant turquoise, which swirls like a great dissolving halo behind his austere head. This is a naked spirituality without a comfortable home and with no rational explanations at hand. It simply *is*, an irreducible presence in the world, as it is also quite beyond it.

And what simply is may have to be at times on the edge, extreme and ambivalent (as, for example, in the austere work of Samuel Beckett or the paradoxical poetry of Paul Celan, which will be discussed in a later chapter). In the heart of the global consumer society the spiritual may have to be discovered through its absence and, therefore, its need. What can I place against the absurd? What can I place against the unutterably futile? What can I place against my own annihilation? These are profound spiritual questions. As psychoanalysis has revealed, the wound may well be the best hurting place to start from. We begin with the despised and broken elements and move from there. This is the *via negativa*. The work of Frida Kahlo is exemplary in this context. In her paintings the traumatic pain within (see Plate 4) is given expressive form and drawing on various traditions – of the retablos votary narrative, of Christ's Passion, of archaic Mexican mythology – taken unapologetically into the culture and, to that extent, understood, integrated and transcended. Through such acts of transformation and imaginative retelling art creates the ever expanding mythology of consciousness; it amplifies and imbues with ever greater significance the daytime incidents and nocturnal dreams of our lives and thus gives our raw and contingent lives depth and resonance.

Shelley argued in his *A Defence of Poetry*: 'Neither the eye nor the mind can see itself unless reflected upon that which it resembles.'[12] The insight is axiomatic. The best resemblances to the mobile life of consciousness are to be found in significant works of art, for unlike theory, speculation and quantification, real works of art actually express the very rhythms of experience. They offer for our contemplation the states of our own inner life. There are places where propositions cannot go but that does not mean those places are permanently out of bounds. The ultimate silence which Wittgenstein[13] felt philosophy had to leave unviolated *can* be penetrated by all the arts. What cannot be *said* through propositions can be painted, danced, narrated and turned into musical sound and verbal metaphor. That is the whole point. The changing life of the spirit can be embodied, shared and developed non-discursively through the arts.

On developing the spiritual in education and culture

How, then, can we begin to reclaim the spiritual dimension in a form that fits the immense complexity of our own times?

Most obviously, and most unobtrusively, it can happen in the many specific moments and encounters that make up the pattern of our daily lives. A moving example here is given by an American professor in his book *The Edge of Meaning*. After an analysis of the painter Vermeer in which the author describes the superlative way in which that painter captures and makes holy the ordinary moments of our engaged perception, he turns to a moment in his own life which involves a remedial girl he is teaching to read. After moderate success, the girl arrives at the beginning of a new term, utterly silent and withdrawn. When the professor asks her what the matter is, she relays that in the holiday two of her relatives had been murdered. The author writes:

> Here is the child beside me, I thought, suffering what no child should suffer. She is a fragment of God's presence on earth, as real and important as any other, calling out for what I cannot provide, what no one can provide. What can I give her? Not my mind, or my professional expertise, or my intellectual life; only my presence, for whatever it might be worth.[14]

Only my presence; that is the most naked form of spiritual life. But that presence – that being for another person – entails a particular kind of engagement with the world. The author modestly finishes his account – and his long study of meaning across symbolic forms – as follows:

> It occurred to me that she might have trouble understanding what reading is because she had never been read to. So in our lessons I began reading to her from her book, then she would read, then I would read again. It became something we did together.[15]

This is Vermeer in language and, even more crucially, the spirit of life in quiet, anonymous, daily action, as elusive and undoctrinal as breath – and as necessary.

But where today, then, can the reflective and spiritual life be nurtured and disciplined? Some rather elusive centres can be located in the shacks, Nissen huts, crumbling outbuildings and damp basements of our consumer society – in some psycho-therapeutic practises, in some art classes, in some fringe studios and occasional workshops, in parts of the developing ecology movement – in the most obscure interstices of the dominant commercial society and our standardizing educational system. The deepening of consciousness and the quiet attending to consciousness manifestly does not lie at the heart of our competitive consumer society, where the all-pervasive iconography proclaims that individuals are no more than what they possess and consume, nor does it belong at the centre of our schools where the pupil is seen as little more than a passive receptacle for a mass of disassociated facts and convergent ideas, to be regularly disgorged against the ticking of the clock. In such a society the steady nurturing of consciousness, the spiritual development of life for its own spiritual sake, becomes, at best, a chosen 'lifestyle' – doing one's own thing – at worst, an embarrassing irrelevance.

If, as Hegel claimed,[16] the highest aim of cultural democracy is spiritual abundance, then something has gone badly wrong. As I argued in the opening chapter, so much of what is fabricated in our commercial culture has only a destructive bearing on our spiritual potentiality. Millions of lives are daily dissipated in the endless simulacra of manipulated desire. In the vast machine of pseudo-gratification every object becomes deprived of its intrinsic virtue: William Blake becomes a plastic bag, Van Gogh a drinking mug, Frida Kahlo a jigsaw. This massive erosion of meaning is deeply repressive of spirituality; it robs it of a public space in which it could be recognized as well as the means necessary for its expression. In this way that which is most deep in us becomes most alien. How, then, can we begin to develop the spiritual in education? I would like to make a few suggestions that follow logically from what I have proposed so far.

If spirituality is a universal element in human experience then we are all implicated and are all responsible for its development. It can no longer be identified exclusively with the world religions, nor any definitive responsibility located there. Its development is one of the great tasks of education as was claimed by Socrates and Plato. If we ask: is it happening? we have no choice but to answer with a resounding no. Yet the absence only points to the need and the repression of a crucial dimension of human experience.

If spirituality concerns the amplification and deepening of consciousness then both the creation and appreciation of art are essential to its task – for the arts provide the distinctive metaphors and technical means for reflecting the invisible life of human experience. Unlike any other symbolic system the arts have the power to disclose the lineaments of being. To engage with the arts is to engage dynamically with the meanings and possibilities of human existence.

Myth would seem to be an essential part of this work. Through myth we can tell the multiple stories of the journeying soul. Again and again, art-makers have drawn on myth to express their sense of life. The teacher has to bring the spontaneous myth-making propensity of the mind to the immense variety of myths now available in our global culture. It is his or her task to bring together the image theatre of the individual soul to the image theatre of the entire culture. Any specific mythical image can be brought creatively inside the field of its archetype. Thus one can work the field of the Nativity, the field of the crucifixion, the field of the resurrection, the field of the unicorn, the field of the Minotaur, the field of the angel, the field of the fool – only to take those elaborated in western culture. There is immense richness in such collaborative work for in the imagination all time is simultaneous and all space metaphorical.

The narratives and images of the world's religions, also, provide essential material for contemplation and re-enactment. This will involve, at times, a delicate conversion from the literal plane to the imaginative, from the realist to the symbolic, from the outer to the inner. A wonderful example of this is provided by the way in which the *mappa mundi* of Medieval Christianity came to intimately resemble the twentieth century mandala of formal inwardness created by Carl Jung (see Plates 5 and 6). Through a strange paradox, the scientifically discredited map of the universe becomes a spiritual diagram of the inner life. The outer becomes retold as the inward. But, in fact, such transpositions are taking place all the time in the symbolic transformations of cultural life. One has only to consider the crucifixion painting of Frida Kahlo (see Plate 4) and to place it in the field of that archetype to see the possibilities of such retelling.

The work of drawing together the spiritual impulses of the student and the spiritual art of the culture, allowing for quiet contemplation and also the most active experimentation, releasing the play of both the conscious and the unconscious, actively develops and deepens the life of the spirit. By the same token it also provides a means of resistance against the tidal wave of symbolic trivia that hourly breaks over our brainwashed heads. In brief, the arts studio can become the much neglected laboratory of the human soul. This is particularly true of the work in auto-biography mentioned at the opening of this book and described more fully in Chapter 5. But such inner development can only be achieved in those rare places where the teacher is given considerable autonomy and where much of the learning is allowed to follow its own restless and distinctive rhythm.

Is this a postmodern account of spirituality?

In his book *After God* the postmodern theologian Don Cupitt writes:

> As God has faded we have found ourselves gradually becoming able to speak of the theologian as a creative worker and gaining the courage to borrow from other traditions. We should stop speaking of other religious traditions as if they are alive and in good health. They are not; they are all declining very rapidly, like Christianity, and all are available to be looted of whatever they possess that may be useful to us in the future.[17]

This is very close to what I have been arguing, although I have been looking at spirituality through the categories of art and education and, as we have seen, artists have been 'looting' Christianity since the time of William Blake for materials to feed the holy imagination. Cupitt continues:

> I am suggesting that we can and should now be uninhibited and eclectic in creating new religious meanings, practises, and narratives out of the materials available to us. The poetical theology will fiction and refiction our religion, tell and retell the old stories. What will make it a *theology* will be its use in helping us to see ourselves and our life with a greater clarity of moral vision, in helping us to be 'easy, going' about the transience of everything, and in showing us how to live ardently.[18]

This, too, seems rather close to the position I am advocating – except where Cupitt uses the words 'religious' and 'religion' I use the words 'spirit' and 'spiritual' and where he refers to theology I refer to a poetics of culture and education. But the outcome is similar, especially in our insistence on creative play with our inherited cultural resources, in the recognition of human transience and with the art of living, not ironically, but ardently.

At the moment, a major figure being reclaimed by postmodernists is the poet-philosopher, Nietzsche, who clearly apprehended the deep dilemmas that now confront western culture, indeed global culture. His prescient work was, in large measure, an attempt to live these dilemmas – at least in the alchemical chambers of his creative intellect – and resolve them with a final affirmation. He saw the problem of nihilism emerging first as a response of a civilization to the demise of Christianity and, then, as a response to the pseudo-religion of scientism. In his prolific writing Nietzsche fought to overcome the trauma of nihilism with a variety of spiritual responses that were set into play by the following six magnetic principles:

1 The will to power
2 Self-overcoming
3 *Amor fati*
4 Living dangerously
5 Eternal recurrence
6 Affirmation of life.[19]

This is not the place to examine these notions in detail, although they have played a critical part in the development of postmodern spirituality, but it may be possible to productively dramatize the spiritual position set out in this chapter – and more broadly in the whole book – in creative and dialectical relationship to them. I would want to place the following five principles in some kind of critical dialogue with Nietzsche's axioms:

1 The longing for existential recognition (developed in Chapter 1)
2 Creativity especially through the arts (evoked throughout the book)
3 Love of another, being present for others
4 Living openly, living Socratically, living vulnerably

5   Acceptance of transience
6   Affirmation of life.

These propositions taken as a whole are, clearly, not Nietzschean, but they are in the radical spirit and tradition of Nietzsche, as is much of Don Cupitt's theology.
So my position has a certain postmodern nature. There are no historical grand narratives marching through the argument and there is recognition of the need for a vulnerable openness, of being present before the world with an unwritten agenda, of the end of systematic religion. And yet . . . and yet there *is* a sense, also, of a *common* human predicament and the possibility of the play of some universals at work – or what might be better termed biological archetypes. Unlike many postmodernists I do not think culture is just a matter of language – of the sign making us, of the word writing us. There is plenty of evidence to suggest that we are creative agents who aspire to love and who long to be recognized, who need to create symbolic worlds, who desire to understand the intricate patterns of experience and who have to face, as creatively as we can, what seems like the inexorable fact of our radical finitude.[20]
In conclusion, I would like to suggest that these seminal principles may constitute some of the key elements in any contemporary consideration of the role of the spiritual in education and culture. Whether they form a postmodern position or not is obviously a matter of definition and, given the nature of the present spiritual crisis, has to remain of secondary importance.

Chapter 3

The rise and fall of the new arts paradigm in education

When I reflect on my own education I am startled by two things: its random nature and its exclusion of the creative arts. My education was so random it excluded all the sciences as well. At the time it didn't matter to me, nor did it seem to matter to anybody else.

When, at the age of eighteen, I was interviewed for a place on the joint Degree of English and Philosophy course at the University of Bristol a concern was expressed by the panel of interviewers – yes, in those days a panel of academics to interview one shy adolescent – that, as I did not have any science credentials, I might not be eligible for a place. Professor Gifford, who was chairing the interview, remarked that he thought that my certificate in religious education, which I had passed at the age of thirteen, was considered nationally to be a science. He telephoned the academic registrar. There was a short whispered exchange. The Professor put the phone down and beamed at me. Yes, he nodded, RE counted as one of the natural sciences. The panel congratulated me and the interview was over. Extraordinary!

But equally quirky was the fact that I had had no experience of any art form either. Throughout the whole of my education, I had never picked up a paint brush, never buried my hands in clay, never touched a musical instrument, improvised a play, composed a poem or moved my body to the rhythms of dance. For the most part I was an insignificant sleepwalker drifting through the dark night of prescriptive education. The paradigm of progressive education described below passed me by entirely. I was living in another country and speaking another tongue.

Perhaps it was this fundamental impoverishment of the feeling life that first drew me as a young man into teaching literature as creatively as I could and, later, into pondering its connection with the other art forms. Certainly, I could see a pattern of connections across the arts which made them into a community: they were all concerned with shaping an expressive medium into symbolic form which, as finished artwork, addressed the human imagination. So it was that I came to be drawn into a debate about the place of the arts in education and its relationship to the culture of postmodernity. I was invited to edit a series of books presenting a unified conception of the arts. On the flyleaf of the first volume it stated that this book 'insists that the arts, seen together, should be an essential part of the national core curriculum now being proposed by the government'.

For a short time, indeed, it looked as though a holistic conception of the arts might enter the world and offer children what I had never experienced, a unified aesthetic education. But it was not to happen. There were advances of a kind, but not the advance that the writers for the series or the writers of the closely related influential Gulkbenkian Report, The Arts in School, were proposing. As we predicted modernism and progressivism were over but, although we could not know it, so was our conception of the new arts paradigm. Politicians were adroitly adapting some of the pragmatic suggestions but, at the same time, ignoring entirely the larger conception of which they were a subordinate expression. Not only that, but the same politicians were ingeniously instituting a nationalized system whereby no further disturbing ideas could easily enter the educational arena again.

Introduction

There has recently been a dramatic shift in the paradigm of arts teaching in British education; I want to suggest that, say, between 1920 and 1980, the arts were predominantly taught under the shaping powers of progressivism and modernism (a curious fusion, but one that can be seen most clearly in the influential figure of Herbert Read) and that since 1980 they have been taught, with huge compromising problems and acute tensions, more and more inside a new paradigm based on a different set of premises, practices and expectations, related to but different from the parallel shift into postmodernism. This paradigm shift (related to thinking in the Education Institutes of our universities) is not to be identified with the atomistic and politically constructed National Curriculum, though many of the elements dislocated from their original meaning are reflected there.

In this chapter I will first consider the nature of paradigms, then outline schematically the old arts paradigm and attempt to define some of the key elements of the new. Finally, I will indicate reasons for believing that while something of value has been achieved under the shaping energies of the new paradigm, the literal and mechanical way it was instituted betrayed the broad sweep of the philosophy, ignored vital principles of creative pedagogy and maimed the holistic perception which lay at the heart of the thinking. The new arts paradigm died in the hands of politically directed bureaucrats who only understood the mechanical and isolated detail and who never once conceived the spirit of the paradigm being proposed. The political implementation was at best half-hearted and partial, at worst, brutal and cynical. In spite of real individual gains, especially in dance and drama, it left arts teachers as divided as ever and the holistic vision of aesthetic education as unrealized as in the earlier progressive–modernist paradigm. This kind of betrayal is, alas, a very old story in the history of ideas. Between the conception and the reality falls the shadow or, in this case, between the idea and the realization came the politician and his ally, the bureaucrat. . . . But let us begin the analysis by first looking at the fundamental notion of paradigms.

The nature of paradigms

What is meant by a paradigm? The first meaning given in the *Oxford English Dictionary* is 'pattern' and that is a good working concept for the kind of constellations of meaning, explosions and reconstellations which I want to examine. By paradigm I refer to a pattern of interlocking categories and assumptions which make sense of the world – or some portion of it – and the way we act in it. In its naive and most common state a paradigm seems inevitable and therefore inviolable, at least to the one who holds it or, more accurately, is held by it. A paradigm seems to denote reality itself; in its naive state it works in the manner of a primitive mythical projection which is further confirmed by the power of collective sanction: *yes, that is how it is.*

What, then, is a paradigm shift? An historian quoted in Thomas Kuhn's *The Structure of Scientific Revolutions* claimed that a paradigm shift was like picking up the other end of the stick: he then went on to offer a more abstract definition. It has to do, he said, with 'handling the same bundle of data as before, but placing them in a new system of relations with one another by giving them a different framework.[1] Of course, in the sciences and humanities there may be the discovery of new data – the discovery of a new planet, the discovery of a new tribe, the discovery of further biblical scripts – but the paradigm shift comes when fundamentally different categories are used to understand the new phenomenon. What is crucial is the conceptual move towards a radically different form of interpretation. Charles Darwin's theory of evolution through natural selection did not invent a new world, it merely interpreted a biological order that was clearly there for all to see through a set of explanatory principles which clashed profoundly with the received and traditionally sanctioned way of organizing and understanding. It was the biological equivalent of Copernicus' astronomical revolution in the seventeenth century. It involved a most disturbing shift from the conception of a divine creation grasped through biblical revelation and the category of final causation to a conception of a natural evolving world understood through the category of efficient causality. As with many profound paradigm shifts many tried with a desperate fervour to bridge the two opposed conceptions but, in this case, there could be no easy reconciliation. Interestingly, Darwin himself wrote:

> Although I am fully convinced of the truth of the views given in this volume ... I by no means expect to convince experienced naturalists whose minds are stocked with a multitude of facts all viewed, during a long course of years, from a point of view directly opposite to mine.[2]

It is precisely that point of view, passionately held over a long period of time and sanctioned by the collective voices of the culture, which defines a dominant paradigm and which, as Darwin could see, was never changed easily. It is not the facts that remain essential, but the categories and related feeling tones through which we see them; and those shaping categories and affective tones can often involve the very centre of our lives. People will die for paradigms and when they shift suddenly there often follows a most acute period of disorientation. That was certainly the case with the paradigm shift from divine seven-day Creation to that of immensely slow biological evolution, seemingly blind and seemingly unguided by any higher cosmic purpose.

One of the peculiar problems of a paradigm shift relates to language and communication. The emerging paradigm has often little choice but to use the old words with a new set of denotations and connotations. This can cause genuine confusion and engender deep suspicion about motives and integrity. When the traditional Christian refers to God he means an objective being who exists independently of all other life; when the radical Protestant refers to God he may denote an inner aspiration towards perfection or wholeness; when the Newtonian refers to space he envisages flat space but when the Einsteinian speaks of it he means curved space. If the contenders in the dispute refer only to the noun – to God, to space – it could well seem that both parties agree when the reality is, of course, that their common language denotes radically antithetical concepts. As old words are used in different ways, as new words are invented or coined, as emerging words are adopted, used in ambivalent or even self-contradictory ways and then further differentiated or simply dumped, communication across the lines becomes hazardous. The frontier between old and new becomes a semantic war zone. At the height of the paradigm shift, characters on both sides can be seen rushing for their dictionaries to demonstrate righteously the definitive meaning of a particular word with its single etymology and, inevitably, its proper received pronunciation, as if all words could actually stay motionless and neutral when worlds of meaning are colliding and veering in still unmapped directions.

In the world of recent arts education – from, say, 1980 to around 2000 – one of the significant 'symptom' words was *aesthetic*. It was a key word of the new paradigm but deeply problematic. When it was used in a positive way by those representing the new paradigm it was liable to be grossly misconceived. It was generally assumed that one was advocating an exquisite but mindless expansion of the nervous system, an egalitarian extension of the Bloomsbury group or the Pre-Raphaelites; Oscar Wilde for the masses. There was some historic justice in this reading. Oscar Wilde and his followers *were* self-conscious aesthetes, and in one dictionary I consulted an aesthetician was designated 'a professor of taste'. Even in many of the serious formulations of the aesthetic through the eighteenth and nineteenth centuries the aesthetic is often confined to the notions of the beautiful and the sublime. Yet the use of the word in the new paradigm, while including both the sense of the beautiful and the sublime, referred more comprehensively to a sensuous mode of intellectual organization which cognizes and makes active meaning; the senses making sense of the world. The heavily congested space that the word had to work in caused intense confusion and even, at times, a kind of crowd hysteria. But such reclamations and relocations of meaning and the anger and disorientation they quickly released were sure signs of a paradigm switch.

What, then, was the new paradigm shift in arts education? To begin to understand that we must first examine the prior model informing the teaching of the arts through the best part of the twentieth century, the progressive and modernist paradigm.

Understanding the old arts paradigm

The dominant practice of arts teaching for the best part of the twentieth century, emerging in the 1920s, possessing a powerful hegemony through the 1960s and early 1970s and gradually crumbling during the late 1980s, was shaped by two strong influences, progressivism and modernism. It was, at heart, a psychological paradigm of the present tense: of personal learning, of immediate process, of sincerity and of spontaneity with as little formal mediation as possible. According to this powerful and animating paradigm the teacher was essentially the releaser of the child's innate creativity through acts of self-expression and self-discovery. Indeed, the term 'self-expression' is one of the key concepts of the old model, as is the related notion 'child-centred.' The titles of some of the dominant literature, taken together, serve to reveal the informing bias of the paradigm: *Child Art* (1936), *Child Drama* (1954), *Development through Drama* (1967), *Growth through English* (1975), *Education through Art* (1943), *English for Maturity* (1967), *The Intelligence of Feeling* (1974). Their proclamation is as bold as it is unambiguous: the arts are committed to a general learning process related to the psychological development of the child. The small preposition *'through'* is to be closely observed, for it was one of the aims of the new paradigm to Tipp-ex out that little word and in the glaring white gap to insert the alternative preposition *'in'*: education *in* drama, *in* literature – for the new paradigm there was to be no quick passing through but more often a staying in, an in-dwelling, a deepening, a cultural centring.

Writing in 1989 about the Schools Council seminal project *Arts and the Adolescent* (1968–1972) an unrepentant Malcolm Ross was to insist:

> We were not after all advocating education in the arts – still less an apprenticeship for school children in the high western

artistic tradition. Real art and real artists were all but incidental to the thesis of human expressivity that the project was advancing.[3]

Ross went on to clarify the project thus:

> It began by accepting that what arts teachers wanted was good: to give children access to their expressive impulses and to help them use them creatively in the interests of personal development. The project did not challenge these assumptions; it attempted to make teacher practice more effective by articulating the theory implicit in it.[4]

In other words, the intention of that project was to make visible the invisible pattern of assumptions which constitute a paradigm in its most naive form; and the unifying concern of arts teachers was, Ross makes clear, the development of expressivity and human personality, not an apprenticeship into artistic tradition, particularly that of our own long, dialectical, western culture.

The intellectual inspiration for the aim of releasing general creativity came not from aesthetics (that was a disregarded and largely unknown pursuit among arts teachers at the time), nor from any particular school of artistic practice, but largely from psychology and, to a lesser extent, sociology. The key personages stalking Herbert Read's *Education through Art* are Freud and Jung; the most important figure shaping the language and argument of Robert Witkin's influential *The Intelligence of Feeling* was Piaget. The crucial shaping figures behind David Holbrook's advocacy of creative writing and its interpretation were Melanie Klein and D. W. Winnicot. The informing language was essentially behavioural and psychological. When I began teaching in the 1960s we were encouraged to use 'stimuli' to release 'responses'. When the work was finished it was judged most often in terms of its personal sincerity and was greeted by a half moral and half therapeutic: 'thank you for sharing it with us'. It was not an apprenticeship into the sustaining tradition of the art form; the work expressed the uniqueness of the self and that was the purpose of the lesson: self-expression. The arts classroom became a kind of encounter group.

Characteristically in 1972 Leslie Stratta, writing about the teaching of literature, could claim:

Reading, especially of literature, presents all pupils with a number of problems. Books are frequently long or longish, the language used, especially of poetry, is often dense and difficult, more so if the work is from the heritage, the vision of life presented comes from the mature imagination of an adult mind.[5]

In the place of adult literature he wanted to develop language 'for a variety of needs and purposes' working through themes, social issues and general projects. If literature was used, it was a means to the theme – the work of the imagination was clumsily decoded as sociology – but, in fact, very little poetry was used (it was too dense and difficult) and virtually no literature from 'the mature imagination of an adult mind'.

Four years before, Brian Way was similarly claiming that the drama teacher's primary aim was not to teach drama but to develop people:

At this stage only the inner circle (of the self) concerns us, as at the beginnings of drama we are concerned with helping each individual to discover and explore his or her own resources, irrespective of other people . . . What is valuable is for each person to discover for himself his own way of doing it.[6]

Consistent with this model of arts teaching nearly all the necessary resources were seen to reside in the natural self, not in the collective culture and not in the specific art form the teacher was claiming to teach. One released; one did not initiate, nor transmit. Not surprisingly in the late 1970s and early 1980s English and drama reconceived themselves as learning media and went across the curriculum.

Exactly the same orientation is to be found in perhaps the most influential volume of the old arts paradigm, Herbert Read's *Education through Art*. In that work, full of insight and hope, Read contended that while the appreciation of painting could be taught, it should not be started before adolescence. In fact, in many classrooms it was never started. This is what he wrote:

But in so far as by appreciation we mean a response to other people's modes of expression, then the faculty is likely to develop only as one aspect of social adaptation, and cannot be expected to show itself much before the age of adolescence. Until then the real problem is to preserve the original intensity of the child's reactions to the sensuous qualities of experience – to colours, surfaces, shapes and rhythms. These are apt to be so infallibly 'right' that the teacher can only stand over them in a kind of protective awe.[7]

As the teacher became the guardian of the child's vision so the aesthetic field of painting was widely viewed as potentially harmful and corrupting, the questionable forces of culture polluting the higher forces of nature.

Teachers of music were slow to enter the progressive paradigm. In 1963 *The Plowden Report* lamented the fact that the planning of music as a creative subject lagged behind work in language and the visual arts and crafts. In 1970 John Paynter and Peter Aston, in their influential volume *Sound and Silence*, set out to bring the dull reactionary tradition of prescriptive music teaching into the progressive movement of child-centred learning. 'If any one aspect of education today is characteristic of the whole', they wrote, 'it is probably the change of emphasis from children being instructed to children being placed in situations where they can learn for themselves.'[8] They evoked the examples of English, drama and the visual arts and drew attention to the work of Herbert Read, Peter Slade (author of *Child Drama*) and David Holbrook. They asked: 'What is creative music?' and answered:

> First of all, it is a way of saying things which are personal to the individual. It also implies the freedom to explore chosen materials. As far as possible this work should not be controlled by the teacher.[9]

But the revolution was not to spread with the speed of fire – or the speed of child-drama or creative writing. Robert Witkin in 1976 in his book *The Intelligence of Feeling* was to record with sorrow that music teachers, when compared to other arts teachers, made few explicit claims to develop individuality and self-expression. He then moved on to welcome the few brave teachers of music who were courageously pointing in the progressive direction:

> They are looking at music as though it never existed before, as though it is something that is made by children. They are

looking at children, at the pace, the rhythms, the melodies, the frustrations, the very harmonics of their existence and the idea is taking hold of them that maybe, just maybe, this is what music in schools should be about. These teachers are seeking to develop in the child true medium control which results from reflexive awareness, the awareness of form and idea in process, in the making.[10]

True to the progressive paradigm music is here conceived not as an artistic medium with an historic identity but more as an ahistorical material to be played with and, inevitably, the emphasis falls on process rather than achieved artwork.

The impeded movement of progressive music was given further support in 1977 by Christopher Small's eloquent *Music, Society, Education*. Small claimed that he was only re-stating what Herbert Read had argued in *Education through Art* and was applying the principles of that book to the teaching of music. He attacked what he called the terrible ubiquity of masterpieces, the domination of the western tradition and the technical convention of the past while insisting on the supreme importance of the art process and the relative unimportance of the art object. One of the great strengths of the book was that, while deeply critical of many western forms and practises, it proclaimed the expressive virtues of African and Eastern music as well as much contemporary music. In this way it greatly expanded the aesthetic field of music and unwittingly prepared the way for the new paradigm which was to value and systematize not only the expressive nature of music but also its cultural and generic character.

All the examples I have given so far illustrate what Marian Metcalfe, in her lucid study of the history of music teaching in *Living Powers; the Arts in Education*, has called 'the late flowering of progressivism in music education'. The next key volume, the influential *A Basis for Music Education* by Keith Swanwick, published in 1979, marked the end of the intense, controversial and short-lived movement or, at least, its transformation into a much wider framework. In this book self-expression was to be denied as the validating principle of music education, creative process was to be placed in a much larger matrix (of composition, literature studies, audition, skill acquisition and performance) and the value of music was seen to lie not in psychology or sociology but in the aesthetic embodiment of meaning and its aesthetic cognition. All the elements of a new paradigm were in place.

It is in the nature of a paradigm when it is in its ascendancy and determining common practice that it will seem inviolable. A paradigm, when internalized, seems not only to propose a world but to be that very world. It possesses an ontological dimension: it becomes the very core of who one is and what one does. A paradigm, in full power, gives the illusion of permanence: *this is how it is and must be.*

When I first began teaching drama I would take into the hall 'a situation' which I relayed to the pupils, I asked them to break into small groups to improvise the situation, I circled round the hall while they did this and then I would invite them to act out the plays; we did this always inside a circle of chairs where the others sat and watched. It was the formula I had been given as a student, it worked very well and as long as I didn't run out of themes and situations (my main dread) I thought I was teaching drama reasonably well. Not being able to locate the excluded, I was quite unable to see the severe limitations of what I was offering, just as the pupils were unable to identify what they were missing. The subject is what the teacher does. It was with a sense of shock that some years later I realized that my teaching had severely excluded almost the whole aesthetic field of drama and that all I had offered, month after month, term after term, was a weekly improvisation lesson. I had introduced only the tiniest segment of a vast circle.

When all the necessary qualifications have been made, when all the exceptions have been generously granted, it would seem that what was true of my drama lessons was true of most other art disciplines at the time: an attenuated practice and a depleted agenda. The task of rethinking it meant first of all declaring war on oneself, of pulling up all the assumptions about culture, about time, about art, and testing their veracity. And then, even more difficult, one had to see what the assumptions blocked out and made inaccessible to the adapted mind. The task was to conceive the arts within a different set of relationships, to envisage an alternative framework, another paradigm.

Of course, under the old paradigm creative work of a high order was released, especially naive (in the best Laurentian sense) work, and much of the teaching was dynamic. But, at a structural level, there was a problem. Because the majority of students had no sustained and conscious access to a living tradition and a repertoire of techniques and exemplars or a language for discussing the intrinsic elements of art, it had no technical or linguistic means of developing what had been experientially released. Much of the practice, like encounter groups and like my symbolically impoverished drama lessons, was doomed to repeat itself, again and again: endless self-expression with little prospect of artistic advance.

This dilemma was an inevitable outcome of an approach which tended to set up the terms 'self' and 'culture' as opposites. Teachers became the frustrated victims of their own false antitheses. 'Process' in drama could not move towards 'performance' because they were conceived as irreconcilable; similarly, spontaneity could not find artifice; nor the trembling self find the culture it needed because that lay on the dark and forbidden side of its own self-description. The very words – culture, civilization, tradition, form, artifice – had dark veins of guilt and unease running through them. The teacher of art was left in an ironical position, even self-defeating, for he had all but to erase the act of teaching as well as his own subject, from whatever he did in the classroom. A paradigm can release, but it can also blind.

The dilemma of the progressive movement is brought out well in the following remark by Malcolm Ross in *The Creative Arts*:

> If we accept the proposition I am advancing here, i.e. that the basis of arts education is self-expression as an essentially intimate act, as immediate and personal way of knowing, meeting criteria determined solely by the subject of such action, then it is perhaps reasonable to make the assertion that arts education is not, in the first place, about art or the arts at all.[11]

At such a point the art teacher becomes a therapist while the discipline of the art disappears into an infinitely tolerant yet hopelessly misguided psychology. On the one side self, on the other art; on the one side expression, on the other tradition; on the one side private, on the other public.

Yet one had only to claim that children are culture-makers by nature, that they are born into history and community, and the old antitheses drop away like dry scholastic absurdities. As soon as the 'I' is seen as part of an inevitable matrix of cultural connections; as soon as culture and self are seen as working in reciprocal relationship, then, conceptually, a shift has been made which allows in all that had been excluded. This is what happened. The return of the repressed suddenly became the animating power of a new configuration. This began to take shape in the early 1980s in a cultural context which saw, paradoxically, the rise of Mrs Thatcher and the emergence of postmodernism. It is to this configuration of the arts in education that we must now turn.

On the nature of the new arts paradigm

The new paradigm, emerging often as an open confrontation with the old, entailed a much more sympathetic disposition to historic culture, to the need for artistic grammars and to the deep symbolic needs of human spirit. It was, at root, an aesthetic paradigm of the embodied imagination. Here I would like to draw attention to three major elements of the paradigm shift. The first relates to the intrinsic value of art; the second to the place of tradition reconceived as the aesthetic field and the third to the idea of the arts as a generic community.

In the new paradigm the arts were not seen primarily as acts of self-expression and psychological adaptation, but as the fine vehicles of human understanding. At their best and most typical they are cognitive to the very core. In their double aspects, of making and of receiving, the arts are in pursuit of meaning. In art what one grasps through the senses is the embodiment of human meaning. The painter Max Beckmann pointed to this vital *theoretical* element when he wrote:

> Everything intellectual and transcendent is joined together in painting by the uninterrupted labour of the eyes. Each shade of a flower, a face, a tree, a fruit, a sea, a mountain is noted eagerly by the senses, to which is added, in a way we are not conscious, *the work of the mind.*[12]

It is this power of cognition, buzzing and tingling through the engaged senses and the imagination, which makes the arts so educationally significant. It is their sensuous mode of operation which makes them stubbornly specific and differentiates them from other forms of enquiry into human existence. Art makes visible the cognitive life of the senses and the imagination. This is their first value; and it is primary and intrinsic. In relationship to music, this is how Keith Swanwick and Dorothy Taylor put it in the 1980s:

What we value in music is ultimately not to do with belonging to a tradition or with self-development, as some have argued, but depends on a recognition that music is one of the great symbolic modes available to us. Initiation into this activity is what we look for . . . the act of shaping music is a purposeful attempt to articulate something meaningful. It need not be complex or profound . . . but it will be expressive and structured and just as 'objective' as the spoken or written word, an equation or a map.[13]

Now, while these aesthetic powers are innate they can only be developed and deepened in relationship to the great art forms which work through the aesthetic and imaginative faculties. In educational terms this requires a creative induction of the child into the living tradition of the art-form. It is not just a question of teaching Shakespeare, Beethoven, Martha Graham, Kurosawa; but more a question of animating the procession of works, genres, techniques, biographies, movements which make up the symbolic continuum I call the aesthetic field. It is a more dynamic concept than tradition and denotes that vital interactive system of allusion, reference and structure in which all art work is necessarily constituted, from the cave paintings to Elisabeth Frink. In the aesthetic field nothing stays still; all is perpetual oscillation and the child's essential creative work should be placed effectively within it. This view, of course, is not out of key with some of the more positive aspects of postmodernism, which was committed to placing modern work in the continuum of all other historic art and promoted the idea of intertexuality and quotation in both the study and practice of art.

And there was a further assumption marking the paradigm change: all the arts belong together as one single epistemic community. It was held that the six great arts – visual art (including architecture and photography), drama, dance, music, film and literature – form a family of related, if largely autonomous, practices: they all work through the aesthetic, all address the imagination, and all are concerned with the symbolic embodiment of human meaning. They are the disciplines of the embodied imagination. Together, in the matrix of the new paradigm, they made up the generic community of the arts.

In might be instructive to conclude this comparison between the two arts paradigms with some clear polarities. I would propose that whereas the old arts paradigm elevated the autonomous natural self, the new insisted on the value of culture; where the old invited spontaneity, the new was committed to the complimentary recognition of technique, control, evolving mastery; where the old paradigm cherished a general transferable kind of human learning, the new was concerned with a fitting initiation into a specific set of practices, an apprenticeship into the grammar of dance, into literary genres, into kinds of musical notation for which there can be no substitute and which may possess no obvious transferability. The commitment is, as I stated earlier, not to an education through self-expression, but to an education *in* the arts which are envisaged as intrinsically valuable.

This vision of arts education historically coincided with a huge period of educational reform. For a very brief moment it looked as though the new paradigm might be realized in the structures of the National Curriculum. But for largely political and social reasons which this book as a whole seeks to define, it was not to be. Now, as I write in 2002, the individual arts disciplines are more apart than they were in the 1980s and the divisions between them are now deeply and uncritically institutionalized for the foreseeable future. The chance of a whole aesthetic education equivalent to an education in the sciences has been lost for some time to come. Now a narrow result-driven specialist cast of mind prevails. So what went wrong?

The death of the new arts paradigm

Of course, as I have implied throughout, there have been some gains in the National Curriculum deriving from the new arts paradigm. The position of dance is now stronger than it has ever been, increasing its number of pupils at all levels of work, from the primary school to the sixth form; drama has connected much more productively with theatre; music and the visual arts have a much more consistently expressive profile and work in relationship to the whole field of their forms. The teaching of English, likewise, ranges more systematically across the field of literature and consistently locates the key place of Shakespeare in that literary continuum. These are achievements and they relate closely to the paradigm shift against progressivism. Yet for the most part the broad challenge of the new arts paradigm has been lost in an educational system which has a very different set of purposes than those proposed by the advocates of aesthetic education under the new paradigm. There are many reasons for this.

First of all at the level of daily practice, teachers of the arts, like all the other teachers in the state sector, have become obsessively preoccupied with a bewildering list of bureaucratic imperatives far removed from the actualities and potentialities of their teaching. Edwin Webb, who wrote the volume on literature in the new arts paradigm (in the Falmer Press Library of Aesthetic Education), describes the present context of teaching as follows:

> Teachers are far too busy. They are beset by needs which are only indirectly associated with teaching itself. Many of these needs relate to assessment and record-keeping. Teachers (and schools) have targets – all of which are set instrumentally, and most of which have to do with 'results'. These results are, allegedly, measurable and result in school tables of achieve-ment. Thus teachers are driven by the needs of assessment to the extent that assessment itself now preponderantly *drives* education.[14]

The pupils, in turn, spend their lives frenetically preparing for assessment or being assessed or waiting to receive the results of assessment – or, of course, being entirely alienated from it and, hence, disruptive or withdrawn. In a milieu of endless testing and instant accountability it is impossible for profound levels of creativity to be released or for artistic work to find its own distinctive shape. Quite simply, the teacher has no time to allow a digression into fresh symbolic ground; even worse, the teacher is too preoccupied with what has to be done next – and next and next – to even notice the true educational opportunity which has been forfeited. In this grey institutional world of delivery and assessment teachers are reduced to technicians, managers of inert knowledge, distributors of pre-selected skills; operators, not educators.

Charles Plummeridge, author of the volume on music for the new arts paradigm, writes of the current state of music teachers:

> There is no room for questioning and therefore the National Curriculum and all that goes with it is taken as 'given'. This is particularly noticeable when teachers gather together to discuss aspects of music education. Conversations are

dominated by the details and mechanics of official educational policy and the plethora of directives. It often seems as if things like attainment targets, key stage statements and programmes of study have come to be regarded as valuable in themselves.[15]

Indeed, of contemporary state schools, one is consistently left with a desolate image of collective mania and spiritual alienation. Underlying all the external changes resides a crass model of economic learning entirely antithetical to aesthetic education. Here the transmission of skills – all of which are seen as measurable, all of which are deemed to be transferable to other tasks – is conceived, without reference to any other philosophy, as the centre of the educational task. Such a conception, recalling the nineteenth century model of drab utilitarianism mocked by Dickens in *Hard Times*, is indescribably narrow. Applied to a computer course it may have a certain validity, applied to the whole of an arts agenda – or to the whole of education – it is scandalously incomplete. It is an instrumental notion of training, not a seminal concept of education, and it is doing untold harm to the teaching of the arts.

Yet the teaching profession as a whole has no broader model to refer to and no direct access to other kinds of thinking. Young arts teachers coming in from the remodelled and financially pinched postgraduate education courses are trained to serve the National Curriculum and little else: they do no philosophy, they do no comparative history of education, no psychology, no grounded work in pedagogy. They are as cut off from their educational traditions as the bureaucrats who churn out the linguistically impoverished documents that flood our schools and education departments. Hence, what we find among teachers almost everywhere is an adaptive pragmatism, a going with the flow: getting the job done, getting the grades sorted and, anxiously, preparing for the next Ofsted inspection. There is no room for charisma, only contracts. No room for radical questions, only ranked percentages. No room for aesthetics, only certificates.

It is not surprising, then, that a holistic concept of arts education failed to materialize. It is not surprising that the arts are *not* part of the core curriculum. It is not surprising that dance remained incongruously within physical education. It is not surprising that the great neglected art form of film never entered the curriculum. It is not surprising that the arts as a generic community of expressive disciplines are more fragmented, divided and ignorant of each other than ever. Nor is it surprising that many of our adolescents are dangerously illiterate in the life of feeling and, therefore, pitifully gullible before the formidable powers of mass seduction that drive and dazzle our consumer society.

It would seem that the idea of the new arts paradigm, like the related concept of multiple intelligence,[16] was an idea out of joint with the managerial and consumer age in which it was born. In which case it has no choice but to wait for a change in the Zeitgeist, to wait for a change in the flow.

At the moment, with the political centralization of power in education and the related demoralization and financial poverty of university Education departments (which in our story of the two paradigms contributed so much to the forging of both new concepts and alternative pedagogy) change may be a long way off. It is pertinent that at the end of his preface to his influential study *The Postmodern Condition: A Report on Knowledge*, published in 1984, Jean-François Lyotard dedicated his study to the Institut Polytechnique at Vincennes 'at the very postmodern moment that finds the University nearing what may be its end.'[17] Certainly, it would seem true that the university Education departments now serve instrumental goals set by the government and no longer have the resources or the will either to offer radical critiques or to forge new pedagogies. In committee meetings across the country so-called educationalists sit like the chained and encumbered inhabitants of Plato's cave. In such blinkered circumstances it is hard to see how further insights into the arts curriculum can be developed.

Concluding note

But why, it may be asked by the sceptic, do the arts matter so much? The question returns me to a proposition central to this book: the arts are vehicles of understanding. Fully conceived they are, in spite of all the counterfeit nonsense that surrounds us, philosophical necessities; no, even more, in the light of our first two chapters, they are spiritual forces of which our consumer culture is in desperate need. Indeed, the insights of the new arts paradigm will be seen to have their greatest pertinence when the full symbolic impoverishment of our present age has, finally, been grasped.

Part 2

The poetics of culture

Chapter 4

The three faces of wisdom

Literature and the arts as radical routes to understanding

Wisdom? It is a gauche term to use in an age of postmodern irony and scepticism. And yet without some sense of justifying value how can one begin to talk seriously about the arts or about education? The last word particularly carries connotations of advance, development, of irreducible value. To educate a person into cynicism or nihilism sounds like a contradiction. Even so, we are deeply uneasy with the notion of wisdom. It isn't employed in our educational documents, nor is it invoked by postmodern academic critics.

My own experience in this matter is ambiguous. When I went to study English and Philosophy at Bristol I chose a joint course because I thought I stood the best chance then of exploring the forms of wisdom open to me. The expectation was, well, inordinate.

From the very beginning my selection of philosophy – the love, study, or pursuit of wisdom' (OED) – turned out to be a monumental error of judgement. Early on in the course I heard of a seminar on epistemology in which a student was asked to disclose one thing that she knew for certain. God', she had courageously answered. Dr Nidditch, her tutor, then asked how she knew God. Through my heart' came the intrepid reply. Dr Nidditch gazed at her for some time then, with a disdainful smile, briefly enquired: 'And in which ventricle may I ask?' Those were the days of late logical positivism. Whenever I even tried to speak about being or consciousness – as I found speaking in groups difficult – I was curtly informed that what I had just said was hon-philosophy'. The words I used, apparently, had no meaning. They were, apparently, private utterances and, unlike scientific statements, apparently, quite unverifiable.

In the first summer vacation, given a free hand to write any essay we wanted, I wrote with a thrilling sense of engagement on the French philosopher, Henri Bergson. When I took the ink-stained essay to my tutor he looked ill at ease and expostulated Bergson! Ah, non-philosophy!' And then, a few days later, catching me on the stairs in the great Gothic tower of the University he gave me back my euphoric affirmations on creative evolution with the grade B minus bracket minus scrawled on the last page. He was a compassionate man. Dr Nidditch would certainly have given it, without further thought, D minus no bracket minus no bracket or have recommended an immediate transfer to theology! When, later, I discovered the turbulent writings of Nietzsche – One must have chaos in one to give birth to a dancing star', I teach you the übermensch. Man is something that is to be surpassed' – I knew I had put myself on the other side of my joint degree for ever. Quite simply, p hook q' and 'what Abbs SEEMS to be saying here is . . .' and 'Ah! Non-philosophy!' could never satisfy my desire for life-understanding and life-connection, however provisional they had to be.

With English it was different. Here my lecturers were under the influence of the critic F. R. Leavis. Dr Littlewood had his photograph hanging like an icon at the entrance to his study. Another tutor gave a lecture lasting one hour reading directly from the text of the Master. This, I felt, was little more than slavish conformity. And much of the discourse struck me as convoluted and thin-lipped – as if living had to be, at every point, a critical matter far removed from the clean bubbling springs of creativity. There was nothing Dionysian here. And yet, in the cramped study of a rather limited conception of English Literature, I found a connection between the notion of culture and the notion of wisdom. This, at least, was seminal.

Whatever was to happen to me later, I was ready to receive the axiom: culture matters because it enhances life – an axiom as old as western culture – and see it as a foundation stone.

Introduction

As the concept of wisdom is not much evoked these days in schools, in universities, or in the postmodern consumer society at large – an English understatement, if ever there was one – I will begin this chapter with a few qualifications and reservations. First of all, I believe wisdom has, in fact, *many* faces. Though three is a sacred number, it is not meant to be definitive. My aim is to delineate and evoke three aspects of understanding and affirmation, three modes of cognitive apprehension that carry with them elements of the numinous and the transcendent. I would, also, like to state at the outset that while I believe literature and the arts serve many purposes – historical, ideological, linguistic, psychological –

their quintessential value relates to what I can only call life-understanding, life-enhancement, life-wisdom. The arts, at their best, deepen and refine our sense of what it means to be alive; they open out existential possibilities for our lives; they invite us to see again free of the grimy occluding stains of habit, free from the easy smears and cheap distortions of received opinion. At times they disturb, even terrify, but they do so in order to liberate, in order to give birth to some kind of insight, some kind of wisdom. This is a most unfashionable view, a view against the flow, but it seems to me, nonetheless, *true*. After all, today's most fierce fashions are nearly always tomorrow's most facile deceptions.

It is my working assumption throughout this book that the arts matter because they serve – at their best – the deep human impulse to understand, to integrate and to transcend; they serve life's ineradicable desire to live more fully, more abundantly. I have always felt that art and, especially, the making of art enables individuals to ratchet up their ephemeral lives to the level of high symbolic adventure and philosophical questing. And I want to suggest throughout the chapter that it is precisely this seminal concern for questing out and life-wisdom that we are in danger of losing entirely in our universities and schools and in those disciplines, like philosophy, psychology and literary study, which should be especially concerned with its nature and application.

This brings me to the subtitle of the chapter: *literature and the arts as radical routes to understanding*. My dominant reference will be to the art of poetry but I will refer in passing to the visual arts, especially to Bonnard and Blake. For I believe, at root, the visual arts – and, indeed, all the arts, as will become clear in later chapters – matter for the same reason: they are in search of life-wisdom and its embodied expression in memorable form.

What, then, are the three faces of wisdom?

The first face I will call the epiphanic. This will refer to the poem – or the painting or work of art – which sings out of affirmation, the moment of mesmerized revelation. It tends to utter its appreciation in the present tense and would have us, as readers or listeners, catch the beauty and incandescence of the thing seen or, rather, witnessed. It is invariably rhapsodic in character and marks a moment of fusion where the quotidian divisions of subject and object are transcended. My main exemplar here will be James Joyce.

The second face, in contrast, is the Socratic. This is the deeply questioning, the frowning face of wisdom. The Socratic is analytical and takes nothing for granted. It strips away the habitual protections provided by collective opinion or cosy subjectivity. It can appear profoundly negative, even destructive, and yet, I will argue, it is one essential means for keeping the mind on high alert, for keeping the truth open, for preventing the descent of original insight or creative perplexity into reductive platitudes and the daily junk mail of clichés. Here I will take the American poet, Emily Dickinson, as my exemplar.

The third face is the prophetic. If the epiphanic and the Socratic tend to work out of the present tense, the prophetic depends on the conjectural power of the future tense and the subjunctive. It presupposes a power to apprehend possibilities not in the immediate push and press of immediate exigencies, but in the future, tomorrow, next year, in a thousand years time, even at the end of time as, conceivably, the universe contracts to its original state. This leap into time future, enhanced enormously by the buttressing grammar of language and tiny conjectural phrases like 'what if', gives us the power of prophecy, of envisaging other universes, of offering hope and desolation, of utopia and dystopia, of distant galaxies and ultimate dust. My main example here will be the poet and engraver, William Blake.

On the power of the epiphanic

Epiphany: the word itself is revealing. It shows in miniature the confluence of the Hellenic and the Hebraic traditions which has driven the creative and turbulent story of western culture. The word at root is Greek deriving from *epiphaneia*, meaning a *manifestation* or a *showing*, and in the Hebraic Christian tradition came to refer to the manifestation of the divine nature of Christ to the Magi who were not kings, as is commonly assumed, but trained hierophants of Ancient Persian religion. In the Christian faith Twelfth Night commemorates this moment of supreme revelation, a moment of divination. However, the word epiphany has evolved during the last hundred years to mark any rhapsodic state of affirmation with a cognitive charge, any sense of often unexpected and almost invariably overwhelming significance felt within the flux and bombardment of daily experience. And, of course, this state relates to many sublime moments of expression in all the arts, until quite recently when there has been, under various vacuous banners, a virtual repression of the affirmative modes of spiritual perception and symbolic formulation. The evolution of the word epiphany marks an important liberation from the conventions and confines of theological doctrine. It was the writer James Joyce who, with his orthodox Catholic background, did much to take the word into a semantic universe of new meanings and possibilities. As a young emerging novelist, during the early years of the last century, from around 1902 to 1904, Joyce was in the habit of scrawling down into his notebook moments which carried a heightened significance. Much later in the novel *Ulysses* the character Stephen Dedalus referred to the author's early devoted gathering of intense impressions as follows:

> Remember your epiphanies on green oval leaves, deeply deep, copies to be sent if you died to all the great libraries of the world, including Alexandria.[1]

The gently mocking note records with wry humour the wisdom of the mature writer looking at the aesthetic preciousness of the young aesthete composing on green oval leaves, deeply deep, and wanting the ultimate accolade of being deposited in Alexandria Library. But there is that word – epiphanies – transposed to cover these new meanings. In fact, it is used earlier by Joyce in his first novel *Stephen Hero*, written in the years 1904–1905, where the hero, representing the author, defines exactly what he denotes by the word epiphany:

> By an epiphany he means a sudden spiritual manifestation, whether in the vulgarity of speech or in a memorable phase of the mind itself. He believed it was for the man of letters to record these epiphanies with extreme care, seeing that they themselves are the most delicate and evanescent of moments.[2]

We have copies in manuscript form of twenty-two such epiphanies scribbled by Joyce at high speed out of a probable original collection of seventy-one. Most of them were worked into his fiction over the years. The very first one recorded reads as follows:

> (in the parlour of the house in Martello Terrace)
> Mr Vance – (<u>comes in with a stick</u>) O, you know, he'll have to apologize,
> Mrs Joyce.

Mrs Joyce – O yes . . . Do you hear that, Jim?
Mr Vance – Or else – if he doesn't – the eagles'll come and pull out his
eyes.
Mrs Joyce – O, but I'm sure he will apologize.
Joyce – (<u>under the table, to himself</u>)
– Pull out his eyes,
Apologize,
Apologize,
Pull out his eyes.

Apologize,
Pull out his eyes,
Pull out his eyes,
Apologize.[3]

The passage enacts a dramatic moment of terror – in its purest lineaments – which came to form part of the opening sequence of *Portrait of the Artist as a Young Man*. Interestingly, two details in the original manuscript are heavily underlined: **comes in with a stick** and **under the table to himself**. In those details must lie the electric charge of remembered terror. Whether this can be named an epiphany or not I will leave open. An epiphany of terror? That seems like a contradiction. Generally the word, even in its post-Christian meanings, denotes a *positive* revelation and a state of affirmation. Thus the following early passage from Joyce's notebook is closer to its current meaning (still to be inserted in most dictionaries):

> I lie along the deck, against the engine house from which the smell of lukewarm grease exhales. Gigantic mists are marching under the French cliffs, enveloping the coast from headland to headland. The sea moves with the sound of many scales . . . Beyond the misty walls in the dark cathedral church of Our Lady, I hear the bright, even voices of boys singing before the altar there.[4]

In truth, many of the early so-called epiphanies of Joyce have little intrinsic interest and are more like hasty notes, memoranda sent by the quick observer giving the key words, situation, characters to the author for working into dramatic form later. Yet it is Joyce who transposed the word *epiphany* and gave it a high place in both life and letters. Nor is it fortuitous that one of Joyce's most moving literary epiphanies comes at the end of the last story in *The Dubliners*, in a story called *The Dead* in which at the climax of the tale the main protagonist seems to dissolve trance-like into the falling snow, into the spectres of the recent dead, into the cosmic dissolution of all things:

A few light taps upon the pane made him turn to the window. It had begun to snow again. He watched sleepily the flakes, silver and dark, falling obliquely against the lamplight. The time had come for him to set out on his journey westward. Yes, the newspapers were right: snow was general all over Ireland. It was falling on every part of the dark central plain, on the treeless hills, falling softly upon the Bog of Allen and, farther westward, softly falling into the dark mutinous Shannon-waves. It was falling, too, upon every part of the lonely churchyard on the hill where Michael Furey lay buried. It lay thickly drifted on the crooked crosses and headstones, on the spears of the little gate, on the barren thorns. His soul swooned slowly as he heard the snow falling faintly through the universe and faintly falling, like the descent of their last end, upon all the living and the dead.[5]

It can be no accident that *The Dead* is set on the Feast of the Twelfth Night – the date in the Christian calendar marking the recognition of the divine by the three wise men. One of the best definitions of the epiphanic moment – one which had an influence on James Joyce himself and his struggle to document the passing moments of heightened significance – was, in fact, offered by Walter Pater where, examining the Renaissance painter Giorgione, he referred to:

Some brief and wholly concrete moment – into which however all the motives, all the interests and effects of a long history, have condensed themselves, and which seem to absorb past and future in an intense consciousness of the present.[6]

He went on to claim that in such exquisite pauses of time we become spectators of 'all the fullness of existence',[7] of the very quintessence of life itself – that is why I referred earlier to the cognitive charge belonging to such high moments of engaged experience. Indeed, it could well be that the Hindu tradition has the best formulation for grasping the axiomatic elements in this experience of 'I being part of the fullness of existence' and it is in the elementary proposition made up of three monosyllabic words: I AM THAT. Pater was writing about the visual arts and he reminds us that some of the profoundest epiphanies have been represented not by novelists and poets but by painters. By Renaissance painters, certainly, but also by many painters in the nineteenth and twentieth centuries.

Of all the painters that come to mind, few reach the sustained rhapsodic level of Pierre Bonnard (1867–1947) and his life long dedication to express his lyrical experience of the immediate phenomenal world in the moist vibrant transformative substance of paint. Bonnard is the patron saint of visual epiphanies. His work was a continuous recreation of daily domestic life through the transformative medium of paint: from his wife Marthe to the bottle of wine, the morning's bread, apples, the domestic spaniel, the light breaking in through the window. Here is the ecstasy of the ordinary. The fullness of existence. The quintessence of life indeed! I have started with the epiphanic mode because its inspiring and central place in the ecology of life and art has been badly neglected. Irony cannot understand lyrical affirmation. So much art, so much writing, has in the last twenty years become sensational in a brutish manner or merely ironic or, the final cognitive evasion of all, merely formalist in execution and self-referential in purpose. Such intimidating fashions, fanned tirelessly by the parasitic media, drain and depress the nation and remove us from the vital naive instinctive sources of art-making and art-responding. At one move they sheer away the affirmative ground of being which it has been one of the functions of the arts to express, symbolize, refine and make collectively memorable.

I want now to turn to the second face of wisdom, a face which is all but the polar opposite of the epiphanic. This is the face of interrogation, of critical scrutiny, of remorseless questioning. It is the Socratic face of wisdom.

On the subverting nature of the Socratic

The word often used for Socrates' method of teaching and awakening was the elenchus. It was as disturbing a discovery as it was transformative. Plato, as a young man, encountering Socrates in the marketplace of Athens, was changed for ever: a brilliant prospective politician under his shaping influence became the first systematic author-philosopher. What was the elenchus that he witnessed and underwent? In English this ancient Greek word means *refutation* and, indeed, that stark word carries much of the import of Socratic philosophy. The aim appears entirely negative: an examination leading towards refutation. The first intention is to destroy the elaborate edifice of internalized opinion that blocks the power of authentic thinking. Thus Socrates works with a teacher's diligence to undermine all the opinions imbibed uncritically, all the thought we have assumed and yet never once thought through, all the propositions we have propounded without prior analysis. The strategy is to destroy verbal reaction and in its dusty ruins to cast the seeds of reflection. Yet reflection can begin in sheer silence, in simply not-knowing, in being dumbfounded, in being utterly speechless. Socrates had such a power to mesmerize and paralyse individuals that he was compared to a stingray.

There is a famous passage in Plato where Socrates compares the method of the elenchus with that of the doctor clearing the blocked system of an ailing patient. In the dialogue Socrates claims that the elenchus is a purification of the psyche. The individual has to be refuted and brought to shame so that the genuine philosophical life can begin. In the dialogue he points out that the movement from crass opinion to critical engagement is in itself a moral improvement of the first order – for a clear openness of mind, free from the delusions of opinion, is 'the most temperate state to be in'. Not-knowing is often, paradoxically, a positive opening, a clearing of the mind, a creative pre-condition for finding out, for the beginning of wisdom. But any subsequent finding out must also bear within it the possibility of falling away and the need for the whole critical process starting again. Once the elenchus has been experienced it will leave its indelible effect. It has the power to question any conviction. It is the enemy of fanaticism, of fashion and of all forms of general linguistic fraudulence. The Delphic Oracle deemed Socrates the wisest man in Athens because he knows he does not know, where all the others claim to know and are, in fact, deluded. Here alertness of consciousness is all.

Now I believe there can also be a *poetic* elenchus. One can write poems which show forth, which linguistically embody, the dramatic fall from meaning and the emergence into new possible meaning. One can have a poetics of creative doubt. A prosody of urgent hesitant enquiry paradoxically dedicated to wisdom, as was Socrates's quest. It is no accident that the very etymological meaning of the Greek word philosophy – *philo sophia* – is love of wisdom. Again, such a conception of philosophy is unspeakably unfashionable, against the flow, but the verbal deposit is there, like a vein of gold, awaiting excavation and fresh manufacture. In the end language games and ideological deconstruction grow predictable and the human being longs for more, for that which hurts and heartens, that which deepens and extends, that which engages the ineffable spirit.

The best way to examine this poetic elenchus – this Socratic mode of poetry – is to see it in action, being used by a great poet. For this reason I want now to consider its operations in the nineteenth-century American poet, Emily Dickinson.

Emily Dickinson was born in America in 1830. She lived nearly all her life in her father's house in Amherst, Massachusetts and became something of a recluse and a dedicated poet. She was enormously prolific. Her whole life was devoted to giving poetic form to the elusive and dramatic nature of her inner experience. In the extreme privacy of her room she explored the predicament of the modern soul and evolved a new way of writing about her experience that was awkward, intimate, radical and often profoundly dislocated. Of the 1,775 poems she composed only a handful were published in her lifetime. She had to wait for almost a century for the strange originality of her idiom to be recognized.

A short aphoristic poem – many of her poems read like aphorisms – written in 1883, two years before her death, reveals the philosophical affinity she felt towards Socrates:

Lad of Athens, faithful be
To Thyself
And Mystery –
All the rest is Perjury –[8]

The intimate address – 'Lad of Athens' – seems doubly right, for the poet is addressing in the cultural conversation that runs down the ages a philosopher she feels a special closeness to, but the address also connotes a kind of radical innocence before the perjury of the common world and the political calculations that secured his death. Furthermore, it is also an abbreviated poetic manifesto: the lad of Athens can be translated into the lass of Amherst for both, in their different ways, were inwardly faithful to the imperatives of their own questing natures inside the perplexing mystery of life:

> Had I not seen the Sun
> I could have borne the shade
> But Light a newer Wilderness
> My wilderness had made –[9]

Emily Dickinson's commitment to not-knowing, to living in the newer wilderness of reflective and unresolved experience, is the explicit theme of a number of her poems:

> This World is not Conclusion –
> A species stands beyond –
> Invisible, as Music –
> But positive as Sound –
>
> It beckons, and it baffles –
> Philosophy – don't know –
> And through a Riddle, at the last –
> Sagacity, must go –
>
> To guess it, puzzles scholars –
> To gain it, men have borne
> Contempt of Generations
> And crucifixion, shown –
>
> Faith slips – and laughs, and rallies –
> Blushes, if any see –
> Plucks at a twig of Evidence –
> And asks a Vane, the way –
>
> Much Gesture from the Pulpit –
> Strong Hallelujahs roll –
> Narcotics cannot still the Tooth
> That nibbles at the soul –[10]

It is clear from the metaphors of the twig and vane that faith is seen here as a refuge, like conventional philosophy, from the tooth that permanently nibbles at the soul. For Emily Dickinson all that we can be sure of is that the world is *not* conclusion, that our experience is unfolding, that it is precarious, that there is often anguish there, as also a sense of something transcendent at work which we cannot easily reach and which overwhelms all definition, though something of it can be caught, as we have seen, in the epiphanic mode of writing. Emily Dickinson reasserts as the modus operandi of her trembling poetry the efficacy of the Socratic elenchus.

It can be seen at work in the following poem, where the claimed certainty of Christian faith is suddenly undercut by the little qualifying preposition 'but', which makes possible a quick transition into its terrifying antithesis:

> I know that He exists.
> Somewhere – in Silence –
> He has hid his rare life
> From our gross eyes.
> 'Tis an instant's play.
> 'Tis a fond Ambush –
> Just to make Bliss
> Earn her own surprise!
>
> But – should the play
> Prove piercing earnest –
> Should the glee – glaze –
> In Death's – stiff – stare –
>
> Would not the fun
> Look too expensive!
> Would not the jest –
> Have crawled too far![11]

The poem has a simple, if fierce, geometry: the first two stanzas utter the collective certainty of Christian faith and her own Nonconformist background, the second two stanzas apply the elenchus of absolute doubt. Should death end our life, making faith's eyes glaze, where then is the promised immortality? This poem, written around 1862 – three years after Darwin's *The Origin of Species* – takes us to the edge of the abyss into which western culture was about to fall. Emily Dickinson provides no answer, only endless philosophical forays, each poem becoming the condition for the next, a dialectical movement of the animate mind, where nothing remains secure except the questing. Each poem seems like a further breathless graphic account of a landscape often impossible to depict where the febrile account can only end, truthfully, with another dash, an incomplete hyphen, leaving space for the next report. Nothing is concluded, except the inconclusiveness. *The wisdom is in the questing.* Not surprisingly, a key word in her inner cartography is not conclusion but *consciousness.*

Yet Emily Dickinson, the Socrates of Amherst, is at her best when she enacts rather than describes or merely denotes her inner experience, when the experience of doubt, of not knowing, of the elenchus is embodied in the pure drama and existential detail of the poem:

> I heard a Fly buzz – when I died –
> The stillness in the Room
> Was like the Stillness in the Air –
> Between the Heaves of Storm –
>
> The Eyes around – had wrung them dry –
> And Breaths were gathering firm
> For that last Onset – when the King
> Be witnessed – in the Room –
>
> I willed my Keepsakes – Signed away
> What portion of me be
> Assignable – and then it was
> There interposed a Fly –
>
> With Blue – uncertain stumbling Buzz –
> Between the light – and me –
> And then the Windows failed – and then
> I could not see to see –[12]

This poem embodies beautifully a dramatic movement from a secure opinion, the expectation of the divine afterlife, to the disturbing actuality of the experience: the uncertain stumbling buzz of the fly leading to the biological/ontological uncertainty of 'I could not see'. The poem expresses through its quick stuttering cadences, sharp images and simple narrative (with its stark juxtaposition) the ultimate state of not knowing.

In the vast, highly erratic urgent jottings of Dickinson there are memorable examples of extreme dislocation, where consciousness is defeated by itself, where any causal meaning or connection eludes the unidentified questing protagonist of the poem. Here we find the experience of Modernism, fifty years before T. S. Eliot's *Waste Land* or Kafka's *The Trial*. This is a form of the elenchus – questioning reason itself and the authority of logic – which even the master, Socrates, did not conceive of. Here are two examples:

I felt a Cleaving in my Mind –
As if my Brain had split –
I tried to match it – Seam by Seam –
But could not make them fit.

The thought behind, I strove to join
Unto the thought before –
But Sequence ravelled out of Sound
Like Balls – upon a Floor.[13]

There is a dynamic subverting life in the mind which the conscious mind cannot fully grasp, which threatens the efficacy of reason and which would appear to render the Socratic faith in logic powerless.

A Thought went up my mind today
That I have had before –
But did not finish – some way back –
I could not fix the Year –

Nor where it went – nor why it came
The second time to me –
Nor definitely, what it was –
Have I the Art to say –

But somewhere – in my Soul – I know
I've met the Thing before –
It just reminded me – 'twas all –
And came my way no more –[14]

Here Emily Dickinson is the poet who acts as sincere witness to the life of consciousness, questioning all collective certainties and charting only the complicated oscillations of ever-changing consciousness. Like Socrates, she was aware of her unique function, of her 'white election'. While holding no public office, while achieving no honours, no recognition, she yet felt called to examine and relay the exact nature of the inner life and set up camp in some of its darker, death-directed, labyrinths.

Like Socrates, Emily Dickinson honoured her god in the only way she knew. The doubt cast by the elenchus was never intended to be a gate into total scepticism, only a clearing of the mind – for the emergence of new being, for the emergence of further truth with its burning light and its great shadow, its dialectical burden, its slant wisdom, its awkward beauty. In following her vocation as a poet she also left us with a new sense of how we might use poetic language to get closer and closer to the perplexing actuality of our immediate consciousness.

On the paradoxical place of the prophetic

The third face of wisdom is the prophetic. If the tenses of the epiphanic and the Socratic are essentially those of the present moment: if the epiphany marks the heightened moment of perception bordering on revelation, and if philosophy marks the penetration of the present tense by the arresting, even paralyzing, power of the question – then the prophetic would seem to depend on a profound sense of time future, of time which is still to come, which has not yet been experienced.

What is incontrovertible is that human beings, and perhaps human beings alone, possess this extraordinary ability to time-jump, a power of imaginative speculation which allows us to free ourselves from the immediate and narrowing demands of biological drive and social dictate. The grammar of the future tense and the subjunctive enable us to leap into possible futures, other worlds, unprecedented possibilities. Yet, of course, one of the sharp spurs for prophetic formulation is often a burning dissatisfaction with the society that surrounds one. This is true of the great Biblical Prophets – Isaiah, Jeremiah, Ezekiel – as it is of romantic and modern prophets. One way of putting it is: if the main instrument for people's understanding of their lives is culture and all the expressive symbols that make up that culture from Dante to Disneyland, from the art of Bonnard to advertisements for beefburgers, and if the dominant culture is essentially corrupt, both limiting and distorting the power and promise of consciousness, then the serious artist, committed to connecting the symbolic life with the life of thought and feeling, can only warn and protest and elaborate alternative mythologies of consciousness. This task has haunted poets from the very outset of the Industrial Revolution from William Blake to Matthew Arnold (consider, for example, his great prophetic poem, *Dover Beach* with its cataclysmic ending), to D. H. Lawrence, T. S. Eliot, Ted Hughes and Geoffrey Hill. In this social context the poet's wisdom is to warn, to sound the alarm, to bang the metaphysical drum. And in this matter there can be little doubt that William Blake, poet, painter, prophet and visionary, is the greatest drummer.

In English literature and in English painting Blake stands like an awkward giant, strange and incomparable, an Old Testament prophet with an utterly modern understanding of the mind and its unconscious tendencies to split and project and repress. Indeed, he could be called the first psychoanalytical theologian in western culture; the man who realized that the devil had possession of, at least, half the truth and wisdom of the world – and nearly all the energy. Artistically Blake's work is uneven, often technically weak, appallingly naive, tantalizingly obscure – inviting far too many academic theses of plausible interpretation – yet the pristine gleam of vision is nearly always there, flashing out of the flawed crevices of the original work. Its inspiration is quintessentially biblical, not classical. At the centre of Blake's elaborate prophetic mythology lies not blind ageing Tiresias, but open-eyed Jesus, the very heart (as Blake saw it) of the human imagination. There is nothing quite like William Blake's images in the whole of Western culture – with their peculiar urgent conviction, with their lineaments of fire, with their graphic linear exactitude. Through his prophetic art Blake struggled to redeem the materialist darkness of his historical period by creating images of spiritual captivity and of liberation. He is the romantic magus bringing not so much epiphanies as revolutionary images of new life, of potential life. His paradigmatic plot is substantially always the same: Albion has fallen because Urizen (reason) has usurped his proper place in the government of the soul and through his ruthless control suppressed other energies essential for wholeness. These other contending energies are named Los and Luvah and Tharmas: intuition, feeling, and sensation. Taken together the characters make up what Blake called the Four Zoas. These four mighty contending energies comprise the explosive diagram of Blake's prophetic imagination.

And here in the dynamic geometry of Blake's work one can glimpse something of the psychological if not the philosophical nature of human wisdom. It would seem to involve in the life of the individual the unification of competing psychic energies. Indeed, the four zoas of Blake powerfully resemble the four dialectical functions of the psyche proposed in the twentieth century by Carl Jung: reason, intuition, feeling and sensation. Part of the wisdom of living consists in holding these conflicting forces in a state of dynamic equilibrium. Blake's diffuse epics can be interpreted as dramas, seeking after the necessary traumatic fall of innocence into experience and pitiful fragmentation, the union of a newly integrated being: namely the individuated self, the mandala self, the whole person.

This utopian icon of wholeness is called by Blake *Jerusalem*. It is an image of the most passionately desired political and spiritual unity which he pitted against both the satanic mills of industrialism and the instrumental mania of dissociated reason. The lyrical poem celebrating the fight for that city in England's green and pleasant lands has entered our collective mythology:

> And did those feet in ancient time
> Walk upon England's mountains green?
> And was the holy Lamb of God
> On England's pleasant pastures seen?
>
> And did the Countenance Divine
> Shine forth upon our clouded hills?
> And was Jerusalem builded here
> Among these dark Satanic Mills?
>
> Bring me my Bow of burning gold:
> Bring me my Arrows of desire:
> Bring me my Spear: O clouds unfold!
> Bring me my Chariot of fire.
>
> I will not cease from Mental Fight,
> Nor shall my Sword sleep in my hand
> Till we have built Jerusalem
> In England's green & pleasant Land.[15]

Tellingly, beneath this his most famous poem, his personal hymn of social liberation, Blake quotes the Old Testament: *Would to God that all the Lord's people were prophets.*[16]

Blake spent his whole life grandly reformulating the mythology he had received to subvert the emerging materialist thesis of his civilization. And yet today, after the bleakest century since the Renaissance, in which visionary politics and symbolic rhetoric led to the deaths of millions, in Germany, in Russia, in Cambodia, in China, such an enterprise has become fraught with dilemmas. It is as if the language of a morally lofty politics expressing a collective vision has become all but unthinkable. We live in the vast shadow of abused archetypal myths; eagles that soared over holocausts, hammers and sickles that fluttered over mass graves. The disturbing truth is that the living image of Jerusalem etched daily on our minds is not that of Blake's at all; it is, rather, today's bleeding city of random carnage, of mindless brutality, of an overarching schizophrenia.

The problem the high prophetic mode leaves us with is the problem of our own politically disillusioned time, where we seem powerless to integrate concepts of solidarity, of beauty and wisdom with our daily lives and with our badly singed knowledge of human nature. It would seem that for the time being the foundations of social hope have been burnt out. It is as if we have all been numbed by the collective high hopes of the last century as we become more and more aware of the huge traumas and unquantifiable tragedies they gave birth to. Yet a postmodern consumer global economy without an inner landscape of the spirit, without a geography of the soul, without an image of the good society, is a nightmare too: a nightmare of mass vacuity, an economy of material success giving birth to nothing but a culture of seduction and betrayal. And there lies our predicament.

For the time being, perhaps, the poet and critic can only warn and offer the most paradoxical insights. The most moving prophet in this context is the poet Paul Celan – a poet I will return to in Chapter 6. He is the singer – and I use that word carefully – of the most searing equivocations and the most poignant paradoxes. Paul Celan lost both his parents in the Jewish Holocaust and, at the age of fifty, committed suicide. Yet, strangely, his poems are not nihilistic. They offer some kind of atonement where atonement would seem to be entirely out of bounds. Celan's poems are small darts of silver hope hurled into a dartboard of despair. They are, in their honed, resonant, elliptical way, prophetic, epiphanic, and Socratic – all at the same moment and against all the odds. They are redemptive aporias:

Psalm
After Paul Celan

No-one can create us again out of the dust.
No-one.

Never.

Hallowed be thy name, No-one.
Who is not in heaven.

Not the Power

Nor the Glory.
For your sake
We live and flower.

We are not roses –
Our stamens broken,
Our stems blood red.

Not in the beginning
Nor in the end.

Flowering now and for never.
Without

Amen.[17]

Conclusion

I have attempted to outline three of the faces of poetry and linked them with the quest for understanding and the task of individual integration. I have suggested that the value of the arts often lies in their power to affirm our being in the world: that feeling of I AM THAT which informs some of our most memorable and cherished experiences and may well possess a deeper sense of understanding, of some unexpected and quite sublime cognition. This facet of art I have called the epiphanic.

But art is also engaged with something else, something more disturbing, more probing, more at risk. It is concerned *not* with the immediate affirmation of existence but with its systematic interrogation. This facet I have called the Socratic and I have tried to bring out the relationship of the open-ended question to the constant act of spiritual questing, for seeking, if not always finding, the truth, of journeying out.

Finally, I have considered the prophetic function. I have suggested the freedom it brings from the airless precinct of the status quo, its capacity to enlarge mental horizons, its power to warn and, at times, to yield hope. Of the three modes I have suggested the prophetic is today the most difficult to employ, at least in its high Biblical and Blakean form.

These three great modalities of art matter because they put us in touch with a desire to understand *philosophically* and to integrate *psychologically*. They also provide the means for directing and deepening the human quest for consciousness. At root the three modalities relate, in complex ways, to wisdom and wisdom I have wanted to say must, against all passing postmodernist fashions, political factions and one-day pragmatisms, return to the very centre of our intellectual and imaginative work – in our universities, in our schools and in our culture at large. It is, of course, an impossible agenda, an agenda against the flow, but, nevertheless, an agenda that must be formulated simply because it expresses the deepest needs of our own etiolated humanity.

Plate 1 Samuel Palmer,
Self-portrait with Aureole.
(1826–1827).
　In this self-portrait painted in
1826–27 we see the individual
artist consciously proclaiming
the role of divine seer,
hierophant of the sacred.

Plate 2 Max Beckmann, *Self-portrait
with a Glass Ball*, (1956).
　The painter holds protectively
the mandala of his own self. He
feels himself committed to the
creation of inner wholeness.

Plate 3 Vincent Van Gogh, *Self-portrait for Gauguin* (1888).

Vincent Van Gogh borrows from the Buddhist iconography to create his own sense of spiritual vulnerability and undoctrinal openness.

Plate 4 Frida Kahlo, *The Broken Column* (1944).

Frida Kahlo uses both images of classical form and the crucifixion to recreate her own sense of dislocation and inner anguish.

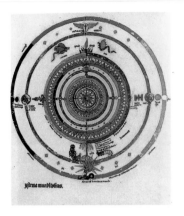

Plate 5 The medieval world-view from the *Liber Divinorum Operum* of Saint Hildegard of Bingen.

This image reveals the medieval view of the world informed by supernatural energies feeding it constantly from without.

Plate 6 Image of Carl Jung's first mandala.

This image of Jung's first mandala reveals the circle as the image of inner wholeness not necessarily dependent on any outer supernatural forces.

Plate 7 Portrait of Marcel Duchamp.

Marcel Duchamp holds one finger to his lips. Perhaps the secret is that he has nothing to say and the enigma is at our expense?

Plate 8 Andrzej Jackowski, *The Vigilant*, (1984).
The compelling cluster of images carry with them deep resonances concerning annihilation and redemption, work and reparation.

▼ *Plate 9* Andrzej Jackowski, *Toxic Tank*, (1996).
Toxic Tank is a version of the holocaust. Contemplating it we become its appalled and implicated witnesses.

▲ *Plate 10* Andrzej Jackowski, *The Boy who Broke the Spell* (1996).
This painting expresses a sense of expectancy, of possible resurrection. It expresses the anticipation of Holy Saturday suspended between the unspeakable Good Friday and the joyous and, perhaps, impossible Easter Sunday.

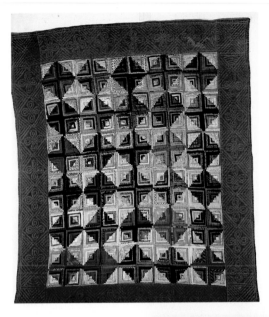

Plate 11 Mary Lloyd Jones' great grandmother's quilt. Between 1850–1900.

For Mary Lloyd Jones, her mother's quilt proclaimed three things: *art belongs where we live and work, it is committed to beauty, it can be made by women.*

Plate 12 Mary Lloyd Jones, *Cwm Rheidol (Scars)* (1993).

The scars of the lead mining of the Rheidol Valley in Wales are recognized and recorded in a painterly gestalt which suggests an enduring natural order that transcends them.

Plate 13 Mary Lloyd Jones *Barclodiad y Gawres* (The Goddess with an Apron-full) (1988).

The gestures are in no way arbitrary; they recreate anew the marks made in Paleolithic and Neolithic times. The images resonate with the signs and signatures of the past. We belong to a wider continuum.

◄ *Plate 14* Harold Mockford, *Night Ferry* (1999).

Anyone familiar with East Sussex in England will have no trouble identifying the actual locations which are the source of Harold Mockford's paintings. This is the night ferry leaving Newhaven.

► *Plate 15* Harold Mockford, *Waiting to go* (1994).

In this painting the sky shifts through three colours not unlike a Rothko painting, except that at the centre there floats two naive clouds taking the viewer away from pure abstraction and locating him in a magical figurative world.

Plate 16 Harold Mockford, *The Ancestors* (1993).

A courageous exploration of inner unease and deep alienation. The painter stands to attention at one side of the painting staring away from the continuity of the generations marked by his dead father sitting in the chair and his grandparents on the wall.

Plate 17 John Meirion Morris, *Modron* (1996).

Here is an archetypal art which has one root in the natural energies of the human mind-body and another deep root penetrating far back into the cultural deposits of La Téne art (500–200 BC) and even further back into the pre-historical.

Plate 18 John Meirion Morris, *Bran* (1993).

The symmetry of *Bran* – a symbolic bird which confronts us with its male and female antinomies – has an almost mathematical rigour based on the sacred number three.

Plate 19 John Meirion Morris, *Trywerin Monument* (1997).

This is engaged public sculpture. It would have us see ourselves not as acquisitive consumers but as threatened historic animals with visionary propensities.

Plate 20 John Meirion Morris, *Trywerin Monument* (detail) (1997).

The bird's beak rises into the higher dimension of consciousness while the great splayed wings bear within them a chorus of shrieking and outraged heads sounding their lament for an exploited culture.

Chapter 5

The creative word and the creative life

A cultural map of autobiography from classical Greece to the postmodern crisis

How old were you?
I'm not sure. About fourteen.
When did it happen?
I'm not sure . . . Around Easter . . . Perhaps later.
Where were you?
*In a seminary. Outside Liverpool . . . At a place called Freshfields
. . . A place for early vocations. The priests wear red sashes round
their waists to show they are prepared to spill their blood for God.*
Anything else?
I'm not sure . . .
What do you remember?
It's the day I have decided to leave the seminary and . . .
And?
*I'm not sure . . . We are ready to file out of the dormitory when the
M.D. – that's the Master of Discipline – one of the priests with a red
sash – he comes in and stops me from joining the others. I'm not
allowed to be with them. To see them. To talk to them. To tell them
that I am leaving . . . I didn't think it would happen like this.*
And then what?
*Then . . . I'm not sure . . . Perhaps I pack my case as he stands there
watching . . . I'm not sure . . . But it's all done quickly . . . And while
the boys are in the chapel or the refectory he takes me through the
dormitory, down the stairs, along the corridor to a back door. . . . I
cannot remember this clearly . . . To see it I almost have to make parts
of it up.*
Well, then, what do you see?
*He is a tall man . . . He is walking quickly . . . He is holding my case
. . . I am almost running . . . running to keep up. I am hoping to see
one of the boys . . . I want to wave to them . . . to let them know . . .*

To tell them I am leaving . . . But there is no one about. Just the silent
stone stairs and the stone corridors and the black flutter-flutter-
flutter of his cassock. And . . .
Yes?
Well that's it . . . Except we come to this side door. It's dark green.
And when he slides it open the light floods in. We step outside. Then
. . . I'm not sure . . . He gives me a ticket, I think . . . I'm not sure
. . . But he hands me the case and then, then . . . without a word . . .
he steps back inside, slides the door and locks it.

Introduction

Writing autobiography as a means to personal reflection and
creativity has become a widely accepted educational practice in
the last two decades. However, the practice has often been
conceived within too narrow a frame, with the result that the work
has often lacked any living connection with a long western culture
of introspective enquiry or any animating awareness of the field
of the autobiographical genre itself. To think of autobiography
and its development is to become aware of a basic principle: that
of *the historicity of the self.* The way in which we habitually envisage
the self – as being inward, with some kind of depth, with some
kind of personal centre – has to be grasped, in large measure, as
a specific cultural configuration, achieved with the greatest
difficulty, often by extraordinary individuals, and in no way an
inevitable part of experience. The self we cherish, if we do, is not
simply given. It has been built up over centuries of cultural labour
and could disappear and possibly is now disappearing, as this
book has constantly suggested, under the impact and demands
of a highly technological and highly standardizing culture. There
have been many societies where the self has not been conceived
as inward and reflective, where it has been seen as determined by
the collective traditions or by the dictates of omnipotent forces
– or both.

It is impossible in a few pages to fully describe the intricate field
of reflective autobiography with its deepest roots in early Greek
philosophy and the early Christian church, but it may be possible
to present historic moments of dramatic crystallization when the
strange quest for individuation took a new turn or a new mode or
manner of expression – or, in the case, of postmodernism, a
startling deconstructive twist. This is what I will attempt in this

chapter, for I believe it is in this ragged historic narrative that we should seek to place, dialectically, our students' autobiographical forays, as well as our own.

There is, though, an acute problem with such an engagement and it is a problem that relates to our postmodern condition. Most postmodernists would deny the very concept of an essential self. For them, following the linguistic turn of philosophy, there can be no foundational self, no essential being to which we can consistently refer or about which we can consistently reflect. In the postmodern paradigm there is only the endless play of different dispersing modes of rhetoric. The postmodern theologian, Don Cupitt writes: 'I am not a sovereign immortal spirit that is or hopes to be self-transparent and self-possessed. All I am is a transient flickering irony that colours the motion of these signs.'[1] Such a conception fits our electronic Zeitgeist and yet, in the long autobiographical tradition of western culture, self-transparency and self-possession have been at the very centre of the enterprise: 'Know thyself and be thyself' said the ancient Greek oracle, as did Plato, Augustine, Montaigne and Rousseau, as did, in their very different ways, Freud and Jung. Thus we stumble upon a kind of aporia: we cultivate autobiography in an intellectual culture which undercuts and makes ironic its deepest purposes.

However, in my experience of this work I have found that the personal narrating of a life is not, generally, a rhetorical diffraction, but more a kind of inner unification, even as it acknowledges painful elements of discord, loss and fragmentation. Perhaps, then, we have to recognize the *historic* truth of postmodernity, even as we struggle for something greater – for it is possible that postmodernity represents just another chapter, a negative but necessary purging, in the long story of individuation. If these propositions have some weight, our educational task may be to hold on to the exacting western tradition of reflexive identity, integrate the current postmodern challenge and then move forward to some further synthesis against the cultural odds. Hold on historically, integrate the subversion and transcend: a formidable task! As far as the making of autobiography goes, this would mean two things: we would have to release a genuine, at times painful and disconcerting autobiographical searching into the personal past and also, simultaneously, a deep excavation into the field of the literary form. The two forces running in parallel should create an animating synergy.

In this chapter I will examine some critical moments in the reflective life of consciousness and in the making of autobiography, for these have been neglected in favour of an all but exclusive reference to contemporary writing. My aim, then, is to offer a working map for the autobiographer and the educator, from the classical time of Greek philosophy to our own unstable post-modern period.

I want to propose that in the western tradition before Heraclitus (*c*.540–*c*.480 BC) the concept of self was essentially epic and tribal and that the Presocratic philosopher Heraclitus marks a key stage in the dramatic emergence of the self, as does the later work of Plato and Socrates and the long 500 year tradition of the Stoics. This classical concern was then deepened by the passionate Christian quest for salvation. It was the Hebraic tradition, in confluence with the Hellenic, which gave birth to the genre of deep subjective autobiography in the form of Saint Augustine's *Confessions* (written around AD 397) – a work that was to have a profound influence on the pattern of self-figuration for centuries until Rousseau's work – also, tellingly, named *Confessions* – written in the middle of the eighteenth century radically changed the pattern of narration and interpretation. This pattern was psycho-logical in manner and it opened the way to a psychological reading of human experience. It gave birth to innumerable 'deep' intro-spective autobiographies and culminated in the twentieth century in the birth of psychoanalysis. Finally, towards the end of that century we witness a crisis in identity, a questioning of the very notion of self. In this crisis the psychological reading of human life is put in radical doubt. The French philosopher Michel Foucault was to write: 'It is no longer possible to think in our day other than in the void left by man's disappearance.'[2] In a similar bleak mood the novelist Elias Canetti was to declare: 'Without noticing it, all mankind suddenly left reality; everything happening since then was supposedly not true; but we supposedly didn't notice.'[3] Postmodern writing – including some autobiographies – set out to systematically destroy what was seen as the comfortable illusion of a continuous identity. This dark void brings us to the present moment.

I suggest that all autobiographers, consciously or unconsciously, willingly or unwillingly, are part of this long tradition and that they can only gain as writers and explorers by a full awareness of it. In this chapter I will present four critical moments in the western story of the self. First, the birth of the notion of the self in Heraclitus; second, the birth of subjective autobiography in Saint Augustine (AD 354–430) third, the birth of a psychological hermeneutics in the sustained autobiographical enterprise of Rousseau (1712–1778) and, finally, the current deconstruction and dispersion of self which can be found in the deliberately dislocated autobiographical work of Roland Barthes (1915–1980).

Heraclitus and the birth of the self

Heraclitus was born around 540 BC and died around 480 BC. He lived on the island of Ephesus and virtually nothing is known about his life. It is clear that he came from a royal family but that he surrendered his hereditary privilege to his brother. He is reputed to have retired often to the Temple of Artemis and to have played dice with the local children, defending himself with the remark that it was better to do so than to engage in political affairs. He is thought to have written a volume titled *On Nature* – but all that remains, possibly from that text, are a number of aphoristic fragments, some of them highly elusive in content, nearly all of them poetic. Some of them are disputed in terms of attribution, others in terms of meaning and translation.

Taken as a whole the fragments express a high disdain for traditional answers and traditional teaching as well as for the vast majority of people who would appear, for Heraclitus, to sleep-walk through life. Heraclitus was reputed to have surpassed all others in arrogance and disdainfulness. His attack on ancestors is particularly significant for it indicates a desire to be free from the accepted conceptions which mark tribal cultures. Critical disdain makes for cultural rupture. It provokes discontinuity. It throws the light of the mind on the immediate moment, the present tense of the 'I thinking its thoughts now', not the high past tense of epic culture and the nostalgic comfort of its formulaic expressions, always anchored in a prior period which was to be admired and emulated. It was in the present tense of philosophy – and, it must be added, in the lyrical poetry of Sappho (*c.* mid-seventh century BC) – that a sense of the individual self came into existence together with a sense of its own strange, unplumbed depths, a sense of a self that could be worked on, explored and developed.

The discovery of the power of critical thought and open speculation involved a profound transformation of human experience.

Heraclitus is at the very beginning of an extraordinary revolution which began to define the role of the mind in the conduct of life. There is an intoxicating element in the enterprise. With a sense of awe, consciousness discovers itself and struggles to speak its hidden and labile nature. In Heraclitus the Greek word *psyche* comes to possess a new denotation and a new set of connotations. It is no longer used – as in Homer – to denote the simple flow of breath or a general life-force, but rather an individual soul which can only be described through the spatial metaphors of depth and inwardness. Here, then, is the origin of the western self with interiority and hidden depths.

In Fragment 71 Heraclitus writes: 'You will not find the boundaries of psyche by travelling in any direction, so deep is the measure of it.'[4] This famous passage depicts a self which is irreconcilable with Homer's epic world. Heraclitus is asserting that the psyche is not physical, is not the flow of breath, but rather an indescribably deep element in individual life. Here is an emergent depth psychology with its own dynamic and dialectic. In Heraclitus psyche has its own logos. It is wholly apposite that one of the shortest remaining fragments of Heraclitus simply reads: 'I have sought for myself'.[5]

In the present tense of early Greek philosophy the formulaic epithets of the earlier Greek warrior culture were breaking down and in their place a more personal and critical orientation to experience was rapidly emerging. After Heraclitus came Socrates (469–399 BC) and Plato (c.428–c.348 BC), the former intensifying the attack on formulaic thinking, the latter offering in Part 5 Book 4 of *The Republic* the first dynamic typology of the self in which the psyche is divided into three, often feuding, elements – the reason, the appetites and the spirit.

Out of this milieu developed the movement called Stoicism, which was to forge an array of practical strategies for the development of the reflective life – including the writing of letters and journals, the memorizing of aphorisms and the emulation of exemplary figures (Heraclitus, Plato, Socrates). Yet the most dramatic development came when this classical tradition met another tradition – that of the Hebraic, especially the early Christian imperative for personal salvation, that intense existential leap out of history – or so it seemed – into the arms of a loving and listening and witnessing God. This called forth a new intensity of inwardness. It also gave birth to the first great subjective autobiography: Saint Augustine's *Confessions*. How was it that Augustine was able to write the first sustained introspective autobiography? What models was he able to draw on? And how was he able to integrate them into a new style of inner exploration?

Saint Augustine and the birth of autobiography

For all the qualifications that have been raised, scholars and literary critics agree that Augustine's thirteen volumes of *Confessions*, written around AD 397, constitute the first major spiritual autobiography in western culture. The essentially linear narrative of the work moves from the birth of Augustine in AD 354 in Thagaste in North Africa, to his conversion to Christianity in Milan, to a mystical experience with his mother at the port of Ostia in AD 387.

The *Confessions* takes the form of an intimate and continuous address to God. All the active verbs in this address involve *utterance*: speaking, confessing, invoking, asking, saying, pleading. The context is one of urgent speaking and listening, not of writing and reading. In the opening paragraph of the work the verb 'invocare', in one form or another, is employed no less than nine times. This speaking out of experience, this pleading before the intimate God who is, at once, most secret and most present, creates a style of writing which is no longer classical.

Augustine speaks in the biblical manner, constantly employing a parataxis with the Latin 'et' to join the flow of feelings, ideas and events. This means that instead of looking down at his feelings from an impersonal distance and soberly placing them in a system of syntactical qualifications, as was the practice of the classical rhetorical traditions, Augustine is able to recreate his emotions from within. He participates emotionally in that which he delineates. The method of parataxis gives him a means of speaking out of his immediate passions so that he is able to dramatize the actuality of his own fluctuating experiences. The heart is Augustine's leading metaphor and parataxis is, as it were, the syntax of the feeling heart. One of the great models for Augustine here was the Psalms – a work which forms a kind of sublime counterpoint running through the whole of the *Confessions* – for the Psalms is also a paratactic monument of praise and penitence in which the voice always sounds like intimate dramatic speech, never like written and complex composition.

At the same time, Augustine is able to draw, whenever he needs to, on the practice of classical rhetoric to dissect and conceptually analyse his interior life. He uses a rich phenomenological method deriving from Greek philosophy to understand the inner turbulence of his own feelings. It is precisely this mastery of two forms of discourse, that of Hebraic parataxis and Hellenic hypotaxis, and the agile movement between them, which enabled Augustine both to narrate his own experience dramatically and to explore its nature and import and in this way virtually to create the genre of subjective autobiography. With the disintegration of classical Latin after his death such an achievement was rendered impossible for centuries.

Through the confessional voice Augustine is, quite simply, able to tell the story of his own life with vivid immediacy. He is able to stop and examine whatever puzzles or perplexes him. He is free to probe whatever state of feeling haunts, torments or mystifies him: grief, love, anguish, inner paralysis, dream sexuality, mystical ecstasy. In Augustine we locate the recreation and scrutiny of inner feeling centuries before the invention of psychoanalysis. But what made this possible? Partly the power to employ two forms of discourse, the dramatic and reflective, partly without doubt, Augustine's own introspective power – but it is essential to notice that the format of the *Confessions* partly derives from common religious practices of Augustine's own historic period: particularly that of the confession, the conversion testimony and the growing habit of self-analysis practised by the desert fathers and the founders of the first monastic orders. Here we find in Augustine both a continuity and a transformation; he internalizes all of these established practices and yet creates out of them, by his own peculiar intensity and his great literary talent, a new literary genre for the amplification of the inner life.

Perhaps, most obviously, the *Confessions* draw on the Christian practice of confession, where the believer brings, through the power of memory, past offences to mind, then analyses through introspection their underlying motives and finally confesses them (often through the gathered community of the early Church) to God in the hope of forgiveness and in the desire for renewal. Often, the confessional ends in a prayer of thanksgiving and of praise. The rhythm of the confessional is the quintessential rhythm of spiritual autobiography. There is a movement of the mind backwards to recall and recollect disorientating fragments of the past; there is an attempt through introspection to understand them and to bring them fully into the present through telling *now* how it was *then*; and, finally, there is a forward movement with a sense of freedom from the past, a feeling of liberation, an enhanced affirmation of what is experienced as the essential self. I have transposed the religious language of the confession into general humanist terms to bring out the autobiographical and therapeutic quality that is embedded in it. In Augustine's *Confessions* this religious practice is transmuted into the most febrile and intimate literature of autobiographical reflexivity and recreation.

We must also bear in mind the methods for self-analysis which the hermits and early monks were developing out of their extreme ascetic lives. Saint Anthony, for example, urged believers to write down their deeds and the movements of their souls in the same manner as they would in confession. This is exactly what Augustine does. He explores the contradictory movements of his soul in a desire to understand them. It would seem almost certain, then, that the long systematic analysis of his spiritual condition towards the end of *Book X* – where he takes each of his senses in turn and adds to the analysis mental curiosity and vanity – derived from emerging practices of introspection within the Christian church of his time though these, in turn, owed much to the tradition of Stoicism. Here, then, was the cultural and spiritual and (as postmodernists would insist) *linguistic* matrix which fostered the development of the inner self through the act of writing.

But there was one further practice which had a direct influence on Augustine's writing: the evangelical testimony. Here Saint Paul – such a crucial figure in the life and conversion of Augustine – is the exemplar. The testimony is an intimate oral narrative in which the protagonist tells the story of his life, often from child-hood to the point of conversion, in order to praise God, to cleanse the soul, and to invite others to participate in the good news. This existential testimony, this telling of a life from the perspective of a momentous conversion, was to exert a profound influence on the western imagination, not only in theology (as it developed into the theory of grace and predestination) but also on romantic and spiritual autobiography, on Rousseau, for example, as much as on Bunyan. The manner of the oral testimony provided a structured narrative with two overt intentions: to tell the speaker's own remarkable story and to influence and convert the listener. It was part of Augustine's achievement to make this oral voice

– the voice of testimony, the voice of confession – a literary voice and in his 'talking' to make fully concrete the life and the feelings he had experienced. By talking about his own existence as dramatic experience he was able to establish the literary principle of autobiography and to extend enormously the range of self-consciousness and the possibilities for self-narration and self-figuration.

Augustine's confessional idiom, then, derived in part from congregational confessions, monastic introspection and the act of giving public testimony of one's own religious beliefs; brought into literature it involved a preoccupation with the minutiae of the inward life, with the hidden life beneath the visible ordinary life, which had not existed previously, certainly not on such a scale or with such subtlety. For Augustine God lies at the centre of the *Confessions*, not the self. Yet his belief in God allows and indeed compels an active exploration into the nature of self. If God is the therapist, the patient can only reach him through stammering out of his own existence – and this is what Augustine does. His belief in God releases a remarkable courage to delineate inner and often contradictory states of consciousness. Like no writer before him Augustine possessed a piercing perception into the depth of the irrational, the power of the demonic and the limitation of the conscious mind either to check or to understand it. His belief in God gave Augustine a kind of strength to define the unstable and destructive elements of his own existence. It also guaranteed a kind of truth-telling. In this way he is able to chart the bewildering and contradictory aspects of his own identity and, at a more general level, to act as a kind of cartographer of inward space, creating a distinctly different philosophy and psychology from that offered by the classical world.

Thus it is that the *Confessions*, written around AD 397, represents an extraordinary objectification of subjectivity. This was not to recur again in western literature until the Renaissance and, in confessional writing, not until Rousseau began to write his equally long and labyrinthine story in 1766. But the aims that Rousseau set himself were to change the form of the literary genre. There was to be a certain continuity, but also a remarkable transformation. What was the nature of the continuity? What was the nature of the radical change?

Rousseau and the birth of psychological analysis

Rousseau's autobiographical work, like Augustine's, is vast, extravagant, contradictory and profound. Rousseau was, all his life, preoccupied with his own self, with his own image, his own inner meaning and with his own deep and ever deepening sense of dislocation from others and from society in general. This preoccupation became virtually obsessional during the last fifteen years of his life. Haunted by his isolation and persecution in 1766 on his visit to England, staying at Wooton Hall in Staffordshire, he began the composition of his *Confessions*. The twelve books took four years to complete and, although he gave readings from them, they were not published in his lifetime.

In a sketch originally intended to form the opening of the *Confessions* and subsequently discarded Rousseau proclaimed the originality of his work. To delineate all facets of his personality; to examine his own behaviour, the sordid and the trivial, as much as the noble and the good; to demarcate an underlying pattern in that behaviour by tracing his own adult dispositions back to their sources in early definitive experience: these are the ends Rousseau consciously set himself and he presented his work as an unprecedented enquiry, requiring a new language:

> For what I have to say it is necessary to invent a language as original as my project. For what tone, what style to take, in order to handle this immense chaos of sentiments so diverse, so contradictory, often so vile and sometimes so sublime, by which I am perpetually agitated? What trivialities, what miseries, will it not be necessary for me to expose. Into what revolting details, indecent, puerile, and often ridiculous, must I not enter in order to follow the thread of my secret dispositions to show how each impression which has made a mark on my soul entered there for the first time.[6]

Yet, ironically, the very same sketch moves on to evoke and apply a traditional paradigm which is central to the mode of its narration. Rousseau himself reveals that his literary creation has a cultural source and that this source was the sacrament of confession:

> I will fulfill rigorously my title and never the most fearful nun will make a more rigorous examination of conscience than I

prepare for myself. Never will she reveal more scrupulously to her confessor all the innermost recesses of her soul than I am going to display to the public . . . I am saying here things about myself which are very odious and of which I have a horror of wishing to excuse myself but also it is the most secret history of my soul. These are my Confessions in the full sense of that word. It is just that the reputation which will follow the work will expiate the sins which the desire to conserve my earlier reputation had made me commit. I wait for public discussion, for the severity of judgements pronounced on high and I submit myself to them.[7]

The writing amply demonstrates that the explicit and tacit conventions of the confession are in full operation. There is the expectation that the person who is confessing will speak the truth; there is the expectation, furthermore, that he will speak from the heart, that he will narrate his mortal sins as well as the venial, that he will accept the judgement conferred upon him and that he will seek expiation. All of these expectations are present in Rousseau's text; at the same time there is also a highly significant secular shift in the convention: Rousseau is addressing his 'odious' actions neither to his confessor nor, like Augustine, directly to the god who created him, but *to the public*. His reader becomes his intimate audience and it is the reader who is given the onerous responsibility of casting judgement. The reader takes on the burden of the priest's office.

In the first volume of the *Confessions* the major 'sins' confessed with difficulty and anguish are, in chronological order, the sexual pleasure derived from Mademoiselle Lambercier's smacking, the theft of the ribbon and his accusation that Marion had stolen it, the insensitive abandonment of his travelling companion Le Maitre when he is suffering from an epileptic fit. In the second volume the major sin, which haunts Rousseau's conscience, is the abandonment of his own children, against the wishes of their mother, to the Foundling Hospital. The confession of one offence makes it more easy to relate another and thus, by degrees, Rousseau in his self-portrait paints the dark and perverse side of his personality.

More than any writer before him Rousseau endeavours to narrate his own weaknesses, his failings, his foibles, his neuroses, his questionable and perverse proclivities. He informs his readers of his pathological shyness, of his habits of masturbating, his occasional bouts of kleptomania, his visit to prostitutes, his act of sexual self-exposure, his complex urinary problems, his exhibitionism, his masochistic streaks. What is distinctive in all this self-disclosure is the author's desire to represent himself faithfully and to do so in the language of psychology rather than the language of Christian piety or theology. Here again one discerns a major modulation of the confessional form, for Rousseau tends towards an understanding of himself in terms of culture and society. To understand the foundations of his personality, he looks to early formative experience, to a complex reciprocal play between natural impulses and shaping environment.

It is in the application of this psychological understanding that the confessional paradigm takes another turn. Rousseau's confession is deeply psychological in its mode of self-analysis and self-revelation. What he is attempting to do is to understand the complex forces which shape human identity; these forces are no longer seen in theological terms but through cultural ones and, furthermore, they are located not in the present moment but in the hidden tangle of past experience.

The analysis is in depth and retrospective. Rousseau offers two remarkable pieces of such self-analysis: one concerns his beating by Mlle Lambercier, the other concerns his premature reading. Both are courageous acts of introspection. No-one before Rousseau had taken intimate childhood experiences and delineated with precision and objectivity their remote and permanent consequences on the life of the suffering dislocated adult. If in Augustine there is a psychoanalysis of feeling, in Rousseau there exist, for the very first time, the very methods of psychoanalysis.

Rousseau's accounts speak eloquently for themselves. Here I will consider only the first account. At the age of eight for some minor offence Rousseau is punished by Mademoiselle Lambercier. At first he is threatened and, then, finally beaten:

> For some time she was content with threats, and this threat of punishment that was quite new to me appeared very terrible; but, after it had been carried out, I found the reality less terrible than the expectation; and what was still more strange, this chastisement made me still more devoted to her who had inflicted it. It needed all the strength of this devotion and all my natural docility to keep myself from doing something which would have deservedly brought upon me a repetition

of it; for I had found in the pain, even in the disgrace, a mixture of sensuality which had made me less afraid than desirous of experiencing it again from the same hand. No doubt, some precocious sexual instinct was mingled with this feeling, for the same chastisement inflicted by her brother would not have seemed to me at all pleasant.[8]

Having described the experience and the kind of pleasure it yielded Rousseau continues by delineating its subsequent and indelible effects. In a comparatively trivial event he sees that a major propensity has been established in his own personality for the rest of his life:

Who would believe that this childish punishment, inflicted upon me when only eight years old by a young woman of thirty, disposed of my tastes, my desires, my passions and my own self for the remainder of my life and that in a manner exactly contrary to that which should have been the natural result. When my feelings were once inflamed, my desires so went astray that, limited to what I had already felt, they did not trouble themselves to look for anything else. In spite of my hot blood, which has been inflamed with sensuality almost from my birth, I kept myself free from every taint until the age when the coldest and most sluggish temperaments begin to develop. In torments for a long time, without knowing why, I devoured with burning glances all the pretty women I met; my imagination unceasingly recalled them to me, only to make use of them in my own fashion, and to make of them so many Mlles Lambercier.[9]

The experience is seen as simultaneously formative and 'deformative'. This is also the case in Rousseau's examination of the effect of early reading upon his life. These acute and detailed descriptions of childhood form the *locus classicus* of confessional writing become introspective and deeply psychological. Given Rousseau's premise that our individual characteristics are largely shaped by early experiences, the art of the autobiographer is not, as in the confessional, to examine the motives as much as to examine the influences of the specific and contingent circumstances on natural impulses. In this way the individual once he has confessed his sins – we would now say traumas – seeks to understand the pattern of social action which brought them about. The autobiographer, to use one of Rousseau's own favourite images, was to become a literary botanist who introspectively examines the phenomena of his own behaviour and, without judgement, attempts to describe and classify it. Here Rousseau's work boldly prefigures the dangerous and difficult self-analytical journeys of Nietzsche, Freud and Jung, and forms a bridge from the eighteenth into the twentieth century.

After Rousseau, the genre of autobiography came of age. Significantly, the actual term 'autobiography' was coined in 1807. Augustine's quest for personal salvation had modulated, for the most part, into the quest for personal individuation; the metaphysical had been transposed into the psychological. In the nineteenth and twentieth centuries many of the great writers wrote autobiographies following the linear chronological form set up by Augustine and Rousseau, but the mode of interpretation was shaped by the seminal example of Rousseau. In the twentieth century the discoveries of Freud and Jung followed in this broad humanist tradition with the key notion of the ego (Freud) or the self (Jung) as the integrating agent in the struggle for consciousness and identity through the reflexive understanding of traumatic experience. Tellingly, Jung was to coin the word 'individuation' to characterize the central task of therapy and in the glossary to his own autobiography *Memories, Dreams, Reflections* was to quote his own definition of the term:

> Individuation means becoming a single, homogenous being and, in so far as 'in-dividuality' embraces our innermost, last and incomparable uniqueness it also implies one's own self. We could therefore translate individuation as 'coming to selfhood' or 'self-realisation'.[10]

It was this coherent notion of a centred life – of coming into selfhood – which was to be subverted by postmodernism. Ironically, it was to be achieved in part with the very language that the psychoanalysts had forged; for the concept of the unconscious entailed that no-one could ever fully know themselves and that many conscious formulations were no more than rhetorical subterfuges cunningly disguising motives we could never be aware of. A radical process of decentring had already started. Indeed, by the end of the twentieth century the original imperative of the Delphic

Oracle – 'know thyself and be thyself' – so powerful a demand in the course of western culture suddenly seemed to be not only demanding the impossible but also holding up a chimera: for, perhaps, there was no essential self to be known and affirmed. Perhaps humankind, and philosophers and writers, in particular, had been duped for centuries by the dramatic illusions cast by the mesmerizing power of language. This was, exactly, what the postmodernists were to claim.

The postmodern disruption

Earlier on in the chapter I quoted the postmodern theologian, Don Cupitt, proclaiming: 'all that I am is a transient flickering irony that colours the motion of these signs.'[11] The signs alluded to here are, of course, the words he is actually using as he writes the proposition. The self envisaged is not, as in the tradition of Christianity and humanism, essential and unique, but rather the construction of words, a rhetorical creation as multiple, ambiguous and unstable as language itself. Such an insubstantial view inaugurates irony – the emotional hallmark of postmodernism – and not vulnerable sincerity, the hallmark of the autobiographical tradition we have been mapping. Expanding on his conception of identity Cupitt writes:

> Consciousness has changed. The older sort of consciousness depended upon a metaphysics of finite and infinite spiritual substances, and upon the notion of pure thought, independent of language and cultural conditioning. But we now see that that spirituality was only ever a rhetorical structure, a narrative constructed within language. This punctures our ancient illusions. We find ourselves obliged to return chastened into narrativity and the flux of linguistic signs.[12]

It is this turn towards language that, above all, marks the post-modern subversion. How are we to understand this dramatic shift of contemporary consciousness with its ironic cast of mind? (Much of this book has been contending, one way or another, with this vexing question.) And what are its implications for the genre of autobiography?

Postmodernism, as we have argued throughout, is now the dominant state of critical consciousness in the western world. It is informed by a number of intellectual movements developing throughout the twentieth century and even earlier (in the writing of Nietzsche, for example), but reaching critical mass in its closing decades. Any inventory of these radically disparate movements would have to include: Thomas Kuhn's notion of paradigm shifts (see Chapter 4), psychoanalysis (especially in its recognition of the unconscious mind), structuralism (originating in the work of Ferdinand de Saussure), post-empiricist philosophy of science (especially in the propositions of nuclear physicists like Heisenberg), Wittgensteinian philosophy (with its notion of 'language games'), deconstructive sociology (here the influence of the work of Michel Foucault has been seminal) and feminism (offering in its various forms a disconcerting reading of western culture as a narrative of repression often linguistically disguised as the quest for rationality and enlightenment). All of these powerful movements gradually constellating in the modern mind created a Zeitgeist profoundly suspicious of all single explanatory narratives, of all encompassing universal meanings, of all under-lying essences.

Symptomatically, many of the key terms of postmodernists begin with the little prefix *de*: *de-construct, de-stabilize, de-centre*. According to the *Oxford English Dictionary* this prefix has 'a privative force' and is used to form compound verbs which have 'the sense of undoing the action of the simple verb or of thereby depriving (anything) of the thing or character therein expressed'. Postmodernism is a privative force in that it seeks to take away the unambiguous authority of any interpretation or any sense of a foundational reality. It undoes the world. As a movement it would open up an uncertain universe without the consolation of final meanings or any ultimate objectivity or grounding. In the matter of autobiography postmodernism would seem to end the tradition of self-knowledge by discarding the very notion of a grounded self, leaving in its absence only the ambiguous traces of language.

The diffracted self: Roland Barthes as autobiographer

One autobiography – or anti-autobiography – that audaciously set up a narrative structure to counter Rousseau's was that of the structuralist, Roland Barthes. It was first published in French in 1977. *Roland Barthes by Roland Barthes* is the title of the work, but the highly visible announcing of the author is deliberately deceptive, a calculated postmodern irony. Any reader taking down this volume from the shelf and expecting an account of the author's life in the confessional and psychological tradition of Augustine and Rousseau would be baffled by what he read. What he would be reading, in fact, would be nothing less than the conscious negation of that literary humanist genre and its expectations. For what Barthes does is to arrange a group of textual fragments under a series of headings according to their alphabetical order. By using such an impersonal method he works to avoid any representation of a single consistent self – such a notion being seen as no more than an illusion, a literary phantom created by the deceptive reifying power of language. His purpose is to deconstruct. He wants to convey in his non-chronological, non-confessional narrative a sense of the arbitrary nature of the self (only a word) and of its multiplicities. 'I am not contradictory', he writes, 'I am dispersed'.[13] The new mode of autobiography – organized by the conventions of alphabetical ordering, rather than the conventions of existential sincerity – in its very structural organization exists to capture the postmodern diffracted 'non-self'.

The sequence of reflections which make up the autobiography often take as their overt theme the disappearance of the self. Under the caption listed under L – *L'ordre dont je ne me souviens plus*[14] – he defends the principle of alphabetical organization as follows:

> The alphabetical order erases everything, banishes every origin. Perhaps in places certain fragments seem to follow one another by some affinity; but the important thing is that that these little networks not be connected, that they not slide into a single enormous network which would be the structure of the book, its meaning. It is in order to halt, to deflect, to divide this descent of discourse towards a destiny of the subject, that at certain moments the alphabet calls you to order (to disorder) and says: *Cut! Resume the story in another way* (but also, sometimes, for the same reason, you must break up the alphabet).[15]

Although there is a mercurial love here of remaining forever unfixed, the essential method is clear as is its declared enemy, *the destiny of the subject*. Under another L reflection, that of *Lucidité*,

Barthes states that he cannot write a book of confessions or aspire to authenticity, for it is no longer possible. Given the splintering categories of History, Ideology, the Unconscious, he claims that he can only be 'open and disjointed', offering no more than text, upon text, upon text 'which never illuminates anything'.[16] Under an N reflection – *nouveau sujet, nouvelle science*[17] – he makes his anti-autobiographical principle transparent: 'he wants to side with any writing whose principle is that *the subject is merely an effect of language*' (my italics).[18] If this was taken as the final word, though Roland Barthes would, no doubt, with his love of paradox disown any such finality, it would constitute the absolute death sentence – in both meanings of the word – of the confessional tradition from Augustine to Freud and Jung.

And yet there is a contradiction at the heart of Barthes' auto-biography. The book is not only composed of text but also of images. The volume opens with a sequence of family-album photographs placed in chronological order, revealing personal and confessional elements, elements of being, elements of exposure, elements of continuity. For example, in one photograph we see a large anxious-looking boy staring apprehensively at the photographer as he hugs his mother. Alongside the image of mother and child the author has written: 'the demand for love'. From another photograph we realize that his father died when he was young. Under another image of himself as a very small child he writes, movingly:

> For it is not the irreversible I discover in my childhood, it is the irreducible: everything which is still in me, by fits and starts; in the child I read quite openly the dark underside of myself – boredom, vulnerability, disposition to despairs (in the plural, fortunately), inward excitement, cut off (unfortunately) from all expression.[19]

What the later intellectual text denies, the images with their highly compressed commentaries proclaim: an individual who lives in time, who has something like an inner life with strong emotional characteristics and propensities, who possesses a dark underside, who is irreducible, who has a certain consistency. 'Everything which is still in me',[20] he writes: but what we need to know is the nature of that 'in'. Here, unexpectedly, almost triumphantly against the major intentions of the author's intellect, we find a return to the confessional idiom: the existential subject, the feeling life, the child in the man.

The photographic sequence belies the intellectual theory. Indeed, as I suggested at the beginning of the chapter, it would seem that we do experience an inner self with certain moods, not linguistically determined, and have enduring and problematic dispositions that transcend their expression in language. Is it not possible that a deconstruction of the deconstructor, Roland Barthes, would reveal a shy boy finding ways of hiding himself in language (when his mother is no longer there) to hold back the world that would snap his subjectivity? In the image the boy would seem to be showing a certain terror before being photographed.

The debate is far from over. But, in the end, it may be *impossible* to have an anti-autobiography which does not reveal aspects of the self, whether intended or not. It is, indeed, impossible to consider human life without a notion of a continuing subject – 'everything which is still in me' – an agent who acts, who writes, who reflects, who edits, who selects, who develops, who experiences, daily, an intentionality which cannot be reduced to the effects of language, who is always more and other than the discourse, who often seeks in language not his own dispersion, but his own idiom, his distinctive way of being in the world, of telling and spelling himself, a subject with a destiny.

If this is so, the development of autobiography will continue to blossom and further forms, integrating and transcending the postmodern challenge, will emerge to startle and amaze us.

The 2,500-year-old story of the psyche is not over yet.

Conclusion

Most of us who write autobiography, who keep introspective journals or who work to develop a reflective disposition towards our own experience, who also work in educational contexts dedicated to this aim, belong to the tradition which has been sketched in this chapter – a tradition that now, paradoxically, includes the postmodern subversion and the postmodern critique. This long tradition has forged the very language we use, post-modernists or not. We are part of its development – even as we turn critically on some of its methods and many of its assumptions. We can only deepen this reflective work by envisaging our endeavours as part of that long adventure, that always unfinished project for human understanding and fulfilment, however broken and uncertain it must now seem.[21] Perhaps, whatever the age, it has always felt something like that to the engaged explorer.

Chapter 6

Music, metaphor, meaning

A poetics before and after postmodernism

There were a few books in my home. In a large gloomy cupboard upstairs, where my mother stored a few tins of peaches, there was a small pile of books covered in dust. I cannot remember all the titles. There was a copy of The Last of the Mohicans, Black Beauty *and* Coral Island. *I do not recall being particularly drawn to them or ever thinking that I wanted the rudimentary stock expanded. They lay dusty lumber, out of reach.*

And then when I was about sixteen everything changed. I started to write compulsively and read whatever I could find. What happened was simply this. My elder brother was at Paston School in Norfolk. He had suddenly come under the spell of an English teacher, a man who he always called Doker – whether that was his surname or nickname I cannot say. But it was this man Doker that had moved his feelings and engaged his sense of language. My brother would come back from school and say 'Well, what do you think of this?' Then he would read a piece of Blake:

> *I wander thro' each charter'd street,*
> *Near where the charter'd Thames does flow*
> *And mark in every face I meet*
> *Marks of weakness, marks of woe.*

Or some lines from Wilfred Owen:

> *It seemed that out of battle I escaped*
> *Down some profound dull tunnel, long since scooped*
> *Through granites which titanic wars had groined.*
> *Yet also there encumbered sleepers groaned,*
> *Too fast in thought or death to be bestirred.*

I listened to the music of the words and my life changed. I had never heard language charged with so much physical energy. The words seemed to be more real, more tangible than any object I might touch with my fingers or any food I might taste on my tongue. They became an all but intoxicating pleasure. Drunk with words I would stand by the sea at Sheringham and shout the lines into the surge and roar of the falling waves.

And so, in response to my brother, in response to Doker, began my love of literature. I looked for books everywhere. I perused the second-hand bookshops in Norwich for hours. My new passion was both compulsive and, as I had neither tutor nor map, indiscriminate. At Major Dunn's, a notorious junk-shop, I purchased for a few pence Plato's Republic, *D. H. Lawrence's* Kangaroo *and some other book so lacking in any kind of memorability that I have long since forgotten its title.*

And then I started to write poetry. I knew, at the time, this was not a passing affair but a marriage for life. The poetry I wrote was little more than a febrile imitation of the literature I was ingesting. As post-modernists would say the language was speaking me; some poems sounded like naive Walt saluting the cosmos, others like the upstart Beats kicking suburban life. Yet through their language I might find my own; through their voices I might find my voice. It was an untutored apprenticeship.

One day I came across Wordsworth's Tintern Abbey. *Moved by its vision of life I tore it out and carried the pages inside my jacket for weeks. I was, perhaps, seventeen. I was, perhaps, beginning to see the need for a poetics.*

Introduction

What might a metaphysical poetry coming out of our age, but not belonging to it, look like? It would be a poetry which, in its own poetic manner, would engage with many of the suppressed elements of our materialist culture. It would relate directly to the inner and primordial and it would aim to address and transcend the glossy pathologies of our postmodern culture, its violence, its alienation, its surfeit, its irony, its unease.

Such a poetry requires a spirit that is at once contemporary and very ancient. In earlier societies the art-maker was often a kind of healer, a shaman who connected different realms, who brought the divine and the profane together, an agent mediating different levels of being. In an age when the art-maker has become more a showman than a shaman we can still draw sustenance and inspiration from this historic source – for it provides a moving paradigm of both the public and metaphysical function of art. At the same time, as poets we have no choice but to live and create in our own historic time with our expanded, if incoherent, knowledge, our own complex history, our own post-industrialist predicament, our own reflexivity, our own spiritual anguish and artistic isolation. This means that there can be little room for nostalgic archaisms or self-conscious resuscitations of lost rituals. Rather, we have to struggle to develop further a radical art – turbulent and questing – in relationship to the severe dislocations of our postmodern culture.

The new poetry would work to express, cancel and surpass the state of consciousness in our times. The metaphysical poem is not a static mirror held up to society, nor the simple or ironic recording of an impression, but more like a vessel in which the hetero-geneous materials of daily experience are placed for their exquisite, if exacting, transformation. The intense heat which makes such transformation possible is provided by the burning coals of the imagination. The driving concern is with the metamorphosis of meaning – with the exploratory advance of creative understanding in and through the power of the poem, in and beyond the age. The energies of the metaphysical poem are neither essentially descriptive nor impressionist but dynamic and prospective, even prophetic – for the aim is the symbolic embodiment of other patterns and constellations of potential meaning. Not, primarily, reflection, but possible revelation; not repetition, but transfor-mation: not sociological symptom but artistic symbol.

The philosophical agenda set by metaphysical poetry cannot stand apart from the actual technical means of composition. The metaphysics and the poetics are different aspects of the same thing. Through the power of its music, through the dialectic of its juxtapositions, through the pressure of its metaphors, through the variety of its registers the poetry comes to enunciate its meanings. Pre-established ideas set to metre, however skilfully performed (one thinks of the tedious poems of the late Auden) is absolutely *not* what metaphysical poetry is about. Such a practice invites cleverness – the verbal display of what is intellectually known in advance – whereas metaphysical poetry is committed to the hazardous creation of new meaning *inside* the poetic medium, within the unfolding dance of its language and the logic of its emerging images. It involves, often, a movement from the known to the unknown, from the circumscribed to the unbounded. It involves a crossing over into new ground that cannot be described in advance of the making of the poem or, where it is complete, its open active contemplation by the reader or listener. Propositions of themselves do not and cannot make poetry. The new metaphysical poetry has all but nothing to do with philosophical systems being given metrical form. Our metaphysics is, above all, exploratory and knows only too well the certainty of uncertainty and the primacy of questing. It is neither classical, nor rationalist. At the beginning of the twenty-first century we experience ourselves as metaphysical beings without doctrinal consolations. There is no definitive system to contain all that we know or that can hold the burden of our deeper ignorance. The form of metaphysics which constructed vast logical systems and neatly placed human life in them is over. Postmodernism here has performed a necessary cleansing. Ours is a metaphysics of the broken middle, of metaphors created like fragile bridges between opposing desires, of provisional concepts, of possibilities, of insights.

How, then, do the key elements of poetry relate to our contemporary and precarious enterprise? Poetry has, at least, two characteristics which are essential to its performance. One is its musicality; the other is its metaphoric nature. I would like to take each of these in turn and connect them to the contemporary poetic task.

The musicality of poetry

There would seem to be a growing recognition that poetry works, in part, as a pattern of sound directed at the acoustic imagination. Yet the power of the Gutenberg print revolution – and now the global computer revolution – has tended to leave poetry mute: a silent, tongueless, breathless thing absorbed by the eyes and requiring for its understanding a private mental transaction. When I was studying poetry at Bristol University the tutor would say continually: 'Look at the words on the page'. I never recall him once asking us to speak the lines, to sing the cadences, to discover the voice of the poem in our own speaking voice, to find the idiom of the poem in the idiom of our own utterance. The words were seen as print-signs addressing the intellect; they were not grasped as acoustic cadences rising on the breath to address the imagination. The Russian poet Mandelstam's notion of poems being exercises for the breath would have baffled my tutor and the academic tradition of silent reading and cerebral judgement in which he had been trained. We did not speak the poem. We did not perform it. We looked at the page and silently read – and then cast final critical judgement through the written word. Ironically, the poems silenced us.

In the nineteenth century Gerard Manley Hopkins – one of the great metaphysical poets in the English tradition – was one of the few poets to grasp what had been lost as a direct consequence of the printing press. As a man he had a deep love of music and as a priest he had a profound commitment to the recital of public prayer. In his letters he argued that poetry should be released from the merely mental performance of the closet. He named poetry 'the darling child of lips and spoken utterance'[1] and insisted that poetry had to be spoken if it was to be fully grasped. 'Till it is spoken, it is not performed', he wrote, 'and if it does not perform it is not itself.'[2]

The letters of Hopkins progressively unlock the inner logic of poetry as a great performing art. Early on in his letters, in relationship to the reading of his poem *The Loss of the Eurydice*, he proclaims: 'Take a breath and read it with the ears'.[3]

Then in a later letter: 'Read it aloud.'[4] And finally: 'It is, as living art should be, made for performance.'[5]

Writing is thus envisaged as a written record of *speech* and the speech is seen as a sequence of musical sound requiring performance for its aesthetic and spiritual understanding. Poetry as performed utterance. The silent black marks on the page are almost the equivalent of the notes of a score which have to be converted into patterned sound for their full meaning to be understood. The music of poetry – the cadences of verbal sound, now clotted, now free, now impeded, now flying and all the time weaving in and out of silence – can give us stirring metaphysical sensations, hints of the Other felt as ice running down the spine. Emily Dickinson wrote:

> If I read a book and it makes my whole body so cold no fire can ever warm me, I know that is poetry. If I feel physically as if the top of my head were taken off, I know that is poetry. These are the only ways I know it. Is there any other way?[6]

One of the aims of metaphysical poetry is to follow Hopkins and take the lyric back to the lyre, to take poetry back to performance, to breath, to the physical play of sound and silence. We should place poetry securely under the sign of Orpheus again. But this will not be easy, for much of the language we need for formal utterance is jaded and anodyne from endless use and abuse. Any immediate verbal music may be entirely counterfeit and more akin to the bastardized music of advertisements than the objective invitations of good art. In a corrupt linguistic culture immediacy of composition is nearly always false, a symptom of the dilemma rather than a creative answer to it. Unlike Shakespeare we have to blot most of our lines, or use the 'delete' key on the word-processor all but obsessively. We have to consciously negate the first clichéd gestures of the lyrical consciousness, the tacky syllables of a commercially tarnished ecstasy. We have to speak *against* the flow of the language, not with it. Thus our music may well have to be experimental, slant, dislocated, strange, and at times on the other side of immediate comprehension. When the language is contaminated artistic naivety is forever out of place. The alchemical transformation required generally involves profound labour and any sudden transcending insight will have to be struggled for tirelessly against the cultural odds: a *work* of art, indeed.

Here we still have much to learn from T. S. Eliot's *The Waste Land* with its fractured structure, its musical and imaginal montage, with its words of healing mysteriously encoded in the ancient language of Sanskrit – Shantih shantih shantih.[7] Tellingly, the English translation of these words would not bear the gravity of their redemptive meaning, no more than the familiar abstract verbs 'give', 'sympathize' and 'control' could stand in for the powerfully emphatic:

DA
Datta . . .

DA
Dayadhvam . . .

DA
Damyata . . .[8]

The music of Eliot's cadences and their hermetic nature remind one of the poet Paul Celan, who in his lyrical poetry struggled to cleanse the polluted language of his Fascist oppressors. In his difficult, deeply musical, poems he all but decomposed and reconstituted the German language in order to express the intimate nuances of his own profoundly oppositional meanings. In an age of global advertising his methods are instructive. Celan uses all manner of daring linguistic devises: inversion, paradox, logical contradiction, repetition, ellipsis, musical counterpoint, savage juxtaposition as well as the typographical dislocation of words. The violent breakdown of conventional language becomes the condition of the breakthrough of emergent other meaning, of new metaphysical sense, of the unsayable virtually being said through the dialectical powers of rhapsodic cadence and fractured utterance.

In some of Celan's poetry the words seem to rise up out of nothing and through a precarious repetition – a kind of nervous introspective testing of the strength of the word – create, for a few magical seconds, a provisional metaphysical world which falls back, inevitably, again into the silence:

> Came, came,
> Came a word, came
> Came through the night
> Wanted to shine, wanted to shine –[9]

His poems are sonar images of tentative flight, of uncertain migration. Celan himself said: 'the poem itself, insofar as it is a real poem, is aware of the questionableness of its own being.'[10] Language, he insisted, had to go through its own lack of answers, through deserts of silence, through murderous speech to find its individual path out. He saw his own best work as going through and returning enriched. It is a metaphysical axiom that the negative is also positive, and mystics know that silence can speak. It was Celan's declared intention to keep the 'yes' and 'no' unsplit.

Our task as metaphysical poets is not dissimilar to that of Celan's. We have to create meanings on the further side of social sense. We have to liberate words from their conventional cages and allow them to make their own journeys out. In particular, we now need to explore the cleansing power of silence in the performance of poetry. Can we bring to silence what the great Gothic cathedrals brought to light, allowing it an immediate entry into the artifice of the building only to spiritually enhance it through the mediation of the manufactured stained glass, *lux* into *lumen*, natural sunlight into spiritual numinosity? Can we use silence in the way that Henry Moore used the empty hole to enhance the three-dimensionality of his sculpture or the way Hokusai used the white emptiness of the canvas to accent the path of a falling leaf or the red massiveness of the sinking sun? In an age of tireless babble and distracting hype is it possible to create poems which draw on the power of silence to create a new kind of beauty and deep metaphysical resonance? After all the semantic contamination, the massive verbal pollution, might this be one way to cleanse language, to restore its original brightness and to disclose its amber-like depths, its translucent historical memory? Can we give readings which, moving between sound and silence, utterance and emptiness, are themselves metaphysical cleansings of words inside the acoustic house of imagination? Might this be part of the public shamanic function of metaphysical art in our time? One of Celan's poems ends like this:

A word – you know:
a corpse.

let us wash it,
let us comb it,
let us turn its eye
towards heaven.[11]

The power of metaphor

The music of poetry has the power to free language from its general bureaucratic servitude to literal meaning and one dimensional denotation. It opens language to the innate creativity of the speculative and questing mind and makes it a prime agent of exploration. In this it joins the other great force of metaphor – for in the act of creating metaphor we carry across meanings, references, associations from one level to another, from one order to another. Metaphor is a major vehicle for metaphysical thinking. In both words – *metaphor* and *metaphysics* – the *meta* refers to a crossing over. Through the creation of metaphor we hold up other intangible worlds for contemplation, for speculation, even for revelation.

Consider Rilke's own brilliant epitaph inscribed on his grave:

> Rose, oh pure contradiction, joy
> Of being no-one's sleep under so many
> Lids[12]

This is a haunting, dialectical, riddle – in which the rose, the most symbolically charged of all our flowers, possesses a significance for beyond any simple reference to the natural flora. Metaphor not only mirrors, it also lifts from one level to another. It is a radical cognitive energy of the restless mind and can move us rapidly from the natural to the historical to the transcendental, including each element as a field of intersecting energy in the final irreducible configuration. Metaphor *is* metamorphosis.

Rilke once gave a memorable account of the function of the artist. He wrote:

> The transitory is everywhere plunging into a profound Being. And therefore all the form of the here and now are not merely to be used in a time-limited way, but as far as we can, instated within the superior significances in which we share. To instate what is here seen and touched within the widest orbit, that is what is required.[13]

He went on to call this the work of the 'continual conversion of the dear visible and tangible into the invisible vibrations and agitations of our own nature'. This profound *instating* is always a re-description and is always dynamic in nature; it is not a naturalistic mirroring, it is an alchemical transformation. Through the imagination the daily substance of our experience becomes spiritual and is taken forward and onwards. Technically we name this astonishing power of poetic instating 'metaphor'. Great metaphors in poetry entail metaphysical acts of connection and expansion which cannot be entirely comprehended by references to the determining forces of nature or history. It is for these reasons that the reception of poetry, as with music and all the other arts, can be experienced as a form of annunciation. An invitation to new life.

If the logos of reason regulates and places and defines; the logos of metaphor deregulates and displaces and offers a migratory movement. A creative diaspora. What is missing in so much contemporary writing is this failure to journey out, to migrate. It is, at heart, the failure to transpose and transcend, to move from one level – to another – to move up (and down) the scale of symbolic meaning. Poems in our age tend to be misty self-conscious mirrors reflecting ephemeral impressions – and are, therefore extraordinarily boring – or blatant lumps of overcooked ideology which stick in our throats as they give us their indigestible 'message'. Too often, contemporary poems are devoid of musical resonance and lack deep metaphor. There often seems to be a general fear of any engaged seriousness – for in our ephemeral culture the metaphysical mind is absurdly dubbed elitist. We prefer to talk about skills and techniques or about 'communication' and markets or about political messages relating to gender and class and race – as if this exhausted the number of themes pressing in on our shaken lives or could ever meet our deeper need to live the full symbolic life. Symptomatically, most of our poetry magazines represent no philosophical coherence. They are, with important exceptions, tiny organs of postmodern market eclecticism: they offer their minimal audiences a mixture of crafted impressions, ironic asides and ideological buzzes.

Conclusion

Poets have to struggle to understand the cultural confusion in which they live but there is no good case – other than the usual pragmatic one of making a short-lived and facile reputation – for coinciding with it. One can insist on a necessary, creative, maladaptation. A stubborn difference. A spirited negation. A counter current. An articulate movement against the flow. Why not? – especially when the poetic imagination discloses other ways of shaping language to incarnate images of being and premonitions of truth all but impossible to express in the current reign of triumphant managerial pragmatism and postmodern eclecticism.

   This, then, is part of the agenda of a new metaphysical poetry. It is in love with the trinity of music and metaphor and meaning. It advocates performance; poetry as utterance. It is always philosophical because it is always in quest. It is committed to an engagement where the aesthetic and the spiritual labour together – an engagement which our glossy standardizing age in its dedication to a vulgar and voracious materialism has, for the moment, all but lost. The poetics is certainly corrective and would seek to be prophetic, yet while it aims to go beyond the status quo of postmodern understanding it does not aim to dissolve our awkward predicament. Paradox marks our lives; opposites war within us and while there may be moments of vision, there can be no finality.

The French philosopher Paul Ricoeur[14] pointed out that when Odysseus completed the rough circle of his long journey home, he returned to confront extraordinary violence and pitiless destruction. The circle cannot be closed. Returning is but to begin again. Here one has to imagine a further fable which, like so many other stories and images, had been swallowed by the indifferent maw of time; in this lost fable Odysseus in his great old age sets out again from Ithaca but his destination is never wholly clear – nor is the final outcome of the tale. The circle has to be left open. And a good poem may end with a hyphen -

Chapter 7

Thirty-nine notes towards a new metaphysical poetry

Tongue-tied

Father, now when I speak, I speak for you.
The silence you maintained could not be kept.
A knife, it spliced our mutual lives in two.
Tongue-tied, we were forever awkward. And inept.
Silence was our dumb inheritance.
The suicidal note passed down to us:
Keep your tongue still. Keep your mouth shut –
Numbing contract of our rural class.
The laconic words were slowly drawled
To dam our thoughts and let the feelings pass.
Nothing. Say nothing. Say nothing at all.
The anger mounting in the throat was swallowed back;
And swallowed back it became all hell to know
What the dumb thing was which choked us so.

The Singing Head

Harsh. And remote. A square for graves.
A mile from Sheringham. The coast road.
Wind warps the hawthorn. Dwarfs the pines.
Brine abruptly burns the memorial rose.
Mother mourns here, planting against the odds.
Over the inscribed slabs gulls rise and scream.
Singed petals scatter across the epitaphs.
The incoming sea's chopped white and green.

Orpheus' head churns in its own blood,
Shudders with each and every turbulence;

Battered, blind, it turns; bobs on the flood:
A severed head that will not sink,
But through the silence and the blood-stained rings
It sings – it sings – it sings – it sings – it sings.

1

Euripides: *What do you want a poet for?*
Dionysus: *To save the city, of course.*[1]

2

At the beginning of the twenty-first century let us set ourselves an impossible task: to join together our deepest aesthetic impulses with our deepest spiritual impulses.

3

What can possibly be meant by insisting that we need a new metaphysical art with which to confront our age? Such a demand certainly provokes an almost instant disbelief, a sense of diffuse anxiety, at times a thinly veiled hostility. Before one has even been offered the chance to explore the terms or to enunciate the hope they offer, the claim has been dismissed as obscure and vaguely reactionary. And yet the philosophical imperative will not go away because of the inconvenience – or embarrassment – it causes, nor does it elect to be placed on the postmodern counter of further options, as if metaphysical art was to be merely itemized as one more possible commodity for our market economy and market culture.

It is true that the word metaphysical has its own specific history and carries assumptions and expectations which may be confusing. The emphasis, therefore, has to be on the new metaphysics or, even better, the new metaphysical, for the commitment is to the activity of the imagination and to a particular form of attention rather than to any object or set of beliefs. The old metaphysics tended to be confined to logical propositions and to the elaboration of complex systems of understanding, often essentialist or supernatural in character. The call for a new metaphysical art – a new metaphysical poetry – is not necessarily bound to any of these traditional endeavours. The demand for metaphysical art is not a rallying call to adopt any prior system of thought or to embrace any particular religion. This is a crucial negative boundary line. An initial act of vital clarification.

4

In the age of postmodernity we have few securities. That has to be not only acknowledged but embraced. Our metaphysical insecurity has to be radically assimilated. It is now part of our metaphysical condition. Ortega y Gasset once said, philosophy begins with shipwreck; so does metaphysical art. Our greatest paradox is this: that we are metaphysical animals without a metaphysical habitat.

5

In a global consumer society is it possible for the poet still to evoke and name further possibilities of being, conjure further patterns of connection, converse with banished angels or repressed demons, cancel and transcend? Or is the poet destined to become an entertainer, a writer of copy, a good careerist, a nicely adapted postmodern person with rather ironic poems standing at the gateway to the supermarket, American Express or McDonald's?

6

We live in a world of two-dimensional gliding surfaces, of constant stimulation and simulation, of quickly rising and fading simulacra. Our fast-moving lives are lived out against a background of global news, eclectic information, musical theme tunes, advertising images and general exclamatory hype. The individual – who is no longer an individual – is born into a verbal and visual maelstrom and dies with it flickering and babbling over his head.

The poems we make and sing must express, in however indirect a way, something of this cultural maelstrom, even as they struggle to point beyond it. They need not be postmodernist – for irony and pastiche cannot take us very far into the hinterland of consciousness – but they must relate to our unprecedented cultural predicament. As poets we have to understand the actual cultural world in which we live but we do not have to coincide with it. The gift of poetry involves prophetic insight and truth-telling. Our task, then, is not to adapt by becoming entertainers and careerist or the writer in residence for Tesco but by forging the necessary antithesis.

7

Sisyphus requires his boulder, Prometheus his eagle, Aphrodite her lover – and Orpheus? Orpheus requires metaphysical anguish to create his life-affirming music.

8

The postmodernists are right in one respect; they warn us of the dangerous seductions of Grand Theory and Master Narratives – for our sense of life is deeply broken and in the age of Internet, video, television and a market-directed global economy there can be no hope for a cultural centre other than that determined by vested interests and multinational companies. For the moment the poet can only occupy the extreme edge, a precarious landscape of shadows where the light is cast by an eclipsed sun. This is not meant to invite despair but merely to urge that we face directly the predicament of poetry and then consider whether the negative can in certain definable ways be redeemed. For on the edges real lives still unfold, and where life unfolds real art can still be created and the spirit, transgressing the repressive materialism of the age, can still darkly flourish. To make the point with an example: I would suggest that there is more fulfilment in reading a new poem to a friend or to a gathering to mark a wedding or a funeral than to have it published in *The Times Literary Supplement* or *The New York Review of Books* where any exchange may well be entirely mechanical and as unreal and as abstract as a small cheque in the post some months later.

9

If the logos of current pragmatism regulates and places and manages, the logos of metaphor and cadence deregulates and displaces and offers a migratory movement out. Pragmatism addresses the functional brain. Metaphor and cadence address the whole imagination. An age of pragmatism without imagination, an age of postmodernism without meaning, is an age without spirit, prophecy or hope.

10

Much of the poetry currently published in England meets the description 'crafted anecdotes' – while much of what is published in America could go under the name of 'uncrafted anecdotes'.

11

Paradoxically, our imperial global Anglo-American language is dull with the glitter of its own decay. In response, the new metaphysical poet might consider the following cleansing strategies: keep faith with the canonical writers of the past, study Homeric Greek, excavate etymologies, embrace threatened languages, practice the fine art of translation, listen regularly to the musical flow of the breath and the beat of the heart, switch off the television, become a votary of silence.
Here lies the beginning of freedom.

12

Any real poetics in Europe – and that is where we live – must be mapped inside a remarkable culture that goes back and back: from T. S. Eliot and Paul Celan and Mandelstam, through Coleridge and Goethe, through Shakespeare and Dante, to Ovid, Sappho and Homer – and to the shamans and myth-makers before them. There can be no escaping the tradition for, again and again, an individual word will carry ancient poetic sediment and one of the poet's tasks – as language is the poet's medium – is to shake the hidden pollen and seeds that lie there, to allow for a new and quite unexpected fertilisation. An endless linguistic resurrection! Not to work the deep geology of language is to fail the medium.

13

During his lifetime the Greek poet Cavafy never offered a volume of his poems for sale; his method of distributing his work was to give friends and relatives the several pamphlets of his poems that he had printed privately and a folder of his latest offprints or broadsheets.

14

What, then, is the failure of most contemporary poetry? It relates to the severe limitations of its demotic idiom. Imagine that the porter in Macbeth has taken central stage and drugged all the other protagonists in the play. What a contraction of language: *Knock Knock Knock* or *Zoom Zoom Zoom*.

15

There are surplus poets and deficit poets. The former increase our awareness of the range and possibilities of life. They bring a richness of metaphor, of new cadence and real meaning, while the latter contract the range, clog the channels of vital cognition, and spawn a self-regarding provincialism of mind.

16

One is haunted by the image of the Greek poet Sappho making her sharp lyrical poetry out of the daily circumstances of her life; out of her inner life of feeling as it unfolded in relationship to her actual life and circumstances. One of the surviving fragments of Sappho reads quite simply:

Day in, day out,
I hunger and
I struggle.[2]

It would seem that out of this daily hunger and struggle – close to music and dance and intimate with the gods and goddesses – issued her lyrical poems.

But, of course, there is nothing vague about such poetic activity. It requires a dialectical cast of mind, bringing together in one manifold contrary dispositions of the psyche. On one side, we have the tranced submission to preconceptual – even prelinguistic – sources of inspiration:

I took my lyre and said:
come now, my heavenly
tortoise shell, become
a speaking instrument.[3]

On the other side of this tranced conversion of music into sound, there is something quite different: a profound application to the craft of poetry, to a body of techniques for rendering experience into memorable forms, into the verbal temples of enduring significance. Sappho in another fragment – she is destined to remain the poet of fragmented melodies and relationships – which gives her a strange unexpected postmodernity – declared:

> *It is the Muses*
> *who have caused me*
> *to be honoured: they*
> *taught me their craft.*[4]

Thus trance and technique, seen as complementary forces of the creative act, are both at the service of the poetic enunciation of life's meanings and possibilities in the encompassing context of an intimate community:

> *Tell everyone*
> *now today I shall*
> *sing beautifully for*
> *my friends' pleasure.*[5]

Here is an image of poetry in action, doing intimate work, heightening experience by creating symbols for it. And in the cultural background – though 'background' is too detached a word – a play of divine forces and dramatic presences. Here is an animated universe reanimated and driven forward both by the rhythmic pulse of the lyric and the elected metaphor in intimate relationship to the drama of life. The image and example of Sappho suggests a convivial poetics – an intimacy in writing out of our lives, a meeting the world with the living word, an existential aesthetics on the edge, with an exploratory commitment to love and friendship and life. Perhaps such values translated into the harsher idiom of our own times could contribute to the renewal of our sad and withered art and foster a new orientation?

17

Sappho's genius: to compose a dictionary of sighs.

18

The nostalgia of the old metaphysics! We are still haunted by the three broken transcendentals: Truth, Beauty, Goodness.

19

To the devil with sociological symptoms; to the angels with transformative symbols.

20

Yet at or near the end of history Sappho cannot be the person she was at the beginning. She has to change – even while her gifts and obsessions remain. The struggle – day in, day out, over so many centuries, over so much conflicting experience, after so much intellectual argument, after so many moral devastations, after so much knowledge – necessitates inner developments of an extreme and uneasy kind. Today the background of the gods cannot be taken for granted and the innocence of sexuality has gone forever. The waters washing the small island of Lesbos are badly polluted and the banner of Lyrical Poetry has been taken down for the international banner of Coca-Cola. Yet Sappho's need for love remains and the loss of the gods creates a new conscious impulse in her for metaphysical grounding. With the postmodern collapse of accepted religious structures and, indeed, all backgrounds this new need has become all but obsessional. Yet she knows she is still very human, very vulnerable, crazy and in quest – and that the power of the word is still there to express and explore her historically unprecendented predicament. For poetry is not so much a criticism of life, as Matthew Arnold claimed, as the creation of life, a means of intensifying, deepening and expanding our existence.

21

In writing a poem an emerging reality is begging to be let in. Offer me a home, it whispers, or else the world will be deprived and your own life will be eternally forlorn.

22

One formula for metaphysical poetry: *Incongruous matter.*
Disjunctive structure. An encompassing frame. The thread of music.

23

There is something else we can learn from Sappho: the musical
power of poetry. Any poetics worthy of the name must include it
as one of the key elements in poetic expression – for much of
poetry's meaning lies in its cadence, in its rhythmic shape as it
leaves the lips and makes its dancing movement into the acoustic
imagination.

One of the fragments of Sappho (quoted earlier) is part of an
invocation to the Orphic lyre to become an instrument of speech:

> *I took my lyre and said:*
> *come now, my heavenly*
> *tortoise shell, become*
> *a speaking instrument.*[6]

An astonishing prayer: to convert music into the cadence of speech.
Yet it is a prayer central to the enterprise of poetry. If there is no
music in a line then there can be no poetry in it either. Sappho's
invocation involves not the *written* word, not the word inscribed
on parchment, but the word that issues from the larynx and the
lips and addresses, not the eye, but the ear of whoever is listening.
In this context the poem is not the words on the page but, rather,
a pattern of spoken sound cast into the acoustic imagination,
beginning in silence and returning to it. '*Listen*,' it says, '*listen:
catch the intonation, hear the weight or lightness of the syllables, feel
the punctuation of the silence, and hear how the silence is altered after the
utterance.*' This is high metaphysical activity, indeed.

24

It is rather similar with images and rhythms. One immediate image
coming into the imagination will often relate to another in the
tradition and both may relate to a single archetypal configuration.
A fusion takes place securing, at once, spiritual depth and a rich
tangle of historical association. One of the tasks of the poet is

to take a particular image into its deep imaginal field and by so doing increase the supply of psychic energy available. Such acts of connection widen our sense of what it is to be human and free us from the worst elements of electronic and commercial culture – the banality of slogans, brand names, jargon, immediate mass-think. In this sense, the poet is a cultural ecologist, a bridge builder, one who draws different worlds together that another harder journey may continue, that the future may not fall into the abyss. The poem is a magnet drawing together in a new forward constellation the complex associations, rhythms, images already often present in or under the culture. Thus the past enters the present and unfolds into the future, a single creative gestalt working through time.

25

Answer to Wittgenstein:
Whereof one cannot speak, thereof one must shape images, metaphors, cadences.[7]

26

Concepts cannot render a living account of our multiform experience. *This* is postmodern truth. Exit the philosopher, chastened. Enter the poet, cleansed.

27

Music is metaphysics. The compelling sound corresponds to nothing that exists in the world. It is new meaning.

28

Poetry's relation to music can be deeply liberating. It challenges us to leap over the inhibitions imposed by materialist ideologies on one side and ironic minimalists on the other. If we ask of a piece of serious music: to what does it refer? We have to reply that, in some quite fundamental way, it does not refer to anything. The music would seem to build its own universe out of its own structural elements, its own expanding grammar. It rises free of all external designation and causal connection. It stands *sui generis*. Yet, at the same time, when we listen to music we invariably have this irrepressible sensation not only of form but also – and simultaneously – of pure value, of pure meaning. It stands outside the empirical world yet it expresses something we recognize and long to recognize. What we experience listening to music defies prepositional definition but it would seem to have much to do with the freedom of the spirit creatively defining its own nature. It is as if, as we listen to music, we are taken inside a spiritual world as it is being created *ex nihilo*. That is the sensation – and it is a metaphysical one.

29

What, then, is being espoused? For Aristotle metaphysics was the study of the human mind which came after physics. But even such open-ended enquiry is not what is sought. The word metaphysical, in its new application, refers to a primary and all but biological engagement with the making of urgent cognitive sense of our lives. It is concerned with ethical dilemma and possibility, with aesthetic value and its widespread negation, with spiritual potentiality and its opposite, that nullification of meaning and being which haunts our lives and is the root cause of much of our terror and anxiety. It refers to the quest for what may (or may not) encompass; for what may (or may not) bear significance.

What for? What ultimately for? That was the metaphysical question which Tolstoy sought to place before his own art and his own age. It is the question which the new metaphysical poet, not necessarily espousing Tolstoyan values, must raise and wrestle with not only on behalf of himself but also on behalf of the times in which he lives – for it is the highest function of art to represent states of being and becoming which have significance for humankind. This redefinition of metaphysical moves us from the security of systems and prescriptions to the art of questing and questioning. It has to be deeply dialectical in nature – but it holds the redemptive possibility of developing a new metaphysical time and space for consciousness. Metaphysical art, then, is a search for *more*, for what has been in a liberal society severely repressed, for what lies beyond the status quo. It offers an invitation for us to become acrobats in a new kind of space, a space yet to be created for our bewildered time.

30

All good poets are kleptomaniacs. They steal to sharpen the resonance.

31

Before the performance of a poem *silence*; during parts of the performance *silence*; after the performance *silence* (enhanced, vibrant, electrical).

32

Music. Silence. Being.

33

A poetics based on the inexpungable sense of presence: *being here, being now, being . . .*

34

Metaphysical thought can take propositional form, but it is essential to understand that metaphysical experience can also be developed and expressed in other ways. In the arts the metaphysical can take sensuous form, exhilarate the body and address the imagination. It can penetrate the tingling nervous system and predispose it towards transformative experiences all but lost in our contracting materialist culture. There can still be metaphysical axioms but there can also be metaphysical cadences, metaphysical tones and textures, metaphysical gestures and images and metaphysical silences. Indeed, the arts are uniquely equipped to take the imagination into metaphysical time/space, to incarnate the invisible, to body forth the levity of grace, the weight of despair and all the states that lie between them.

35

Move, dialectically: conceive poetry as essential to the fabric of our daily intimate lives and yet, at the same time, root it fiercely in the transcendent and Other. Drive these two energies together until they become one force, one reality, a lived poetics.

36

AXIOM
The aim of culture is to deepen the life of the spirit.
CONCLUSION
A revolution is required.

37

By some paradoxical quirk relating to the innate restlessness of the mind, consciousness is always tending towards its opposite state. After postmodernism and pragmatism, then, a kind of metaphysics; after the reign of the low demotic, the return of metaphor and cadence; after the cult of literal surfaces, the return of imagination. Is it possible that in the dawn light away from the media's microphones and cameras, beyond the electronic babble, someone somewhere is picking up the discarded flute of Orpheus and beginning to play again?
Listen . . .

38

Recent chaos theory claims that a fragile butterfly flying over some remote ocean can, by opening and closing its wings, effect a cleansing storm a thousand miles away. Buddhists, for centuries, have held a similar belief. In that spirit, let us begin . . .

39

Euripides: *What do you want a poet for?*
Dionysus: *To save the city, of course.*[8]

Chapter 8

Art against the Zeitgeist
On the work of four contemporary art-makers

It was the Autumn of 1997; 29 October to be exact. It was the day three of us – a young artist, a teacher of dance and myself – decided to protest against the Turner Prize on the day of its opening at the Tate. We had already sent a letter to Sir Serota asking him to resign. 'This man was hired to depress art', said William Blake of Sir Joshua Reynolds; I felt the same remark could be applied, without qualification, to Sir Serota. Our letter began: 'As director of the Tate Gallery and permanent Chairman of the Turner Prize you preside over a monster which, year after year, with few exceptions, tramples on art and progressively muddies artistic judgement.' At the end of the letter we demanded his instant resignation.

Predictably, on the Monday before the Wednesday, The Times wrote with characteristic hyperbole: 'A gang of angry artists plan to demonstrate on the steps of the Tate . . . and demand Serota's resignation. And they are prepared for a fight.' As the critic Karl Kraus once pointed out: 'events no longer happen, instead the clichés operate spontaneously.' In a sense, our protest was over before it had happened.

Nevertheless, on the Wednesday the three of us arrived at the Tate as the gates were opening. To my amazement at the top of the steps stood a line of bouncers, all bulky men with short hair, all wearing well knotted ties and dark suits. As we walked up the steps with our leaflets, so the bouncers systematically descended.

'Not here', they said, 'it is against the law'. At once we questioned the command. 'On whose authority?' we asked. But our question went unanswered. 'Not on the steps', the bouncers repeated and, pointing back to the road, added: 'On the other side of the gates.'

Before such a display of physical strength, we had little choice. We retreated as they followed us down to the iron gates. There on the pavement we began to give out our leaflets and call for the resignation of Sir Serota. Facing us, for at least an hour, was a plain-clothes policeman.

He refused to answer our spirited 'Good morning' just as he refused to take the broadside we handed him. Instead, with his mobile phone he remained in constant communication with his doppelganger sitting on the bench at the top of the Tate steps. Clearly they were still expecting an unruly gang of artists, emerging from the side streets, 'ready for a fight'. How they overestimated the vitality of British intellectual life! They must have been disappointed.

A small climax came when one of the secretaries working for the Tate came nervously down the steps and asked for a copy of the leaflet. I smuggled her a copy through the black metal railing of the fence and she hurried back into the darkness of the Tate with the paper fluttering in her hands. At least somebody inside the Avant-Garde Fortress wanted to know what someone was thinking outside in the larger world.

Such was our 'mass picket' and storming of the Tate. It was almost my first experience of public protest. I had not been brought up to demonstrate. Three of us had for a short time induced a shudder of alarm in the Visual Art Establishment of Great Britain. That was satisfying – though I much preferred the apocalyptic account given in The Times.

When on 20 November Sir Serota finally replied to our letter we had to smile. For here was the revolutionary Turk of the Tate writing: 'As well as honouring the best of contemporary art the price (sic) has served to generate interest in the work of Britain's living artists more broadly. The debates and conference organized each year also serve that purpose. Yours sincerely, Nicholas Serota. Director.'

It seemed to me, in the light of this bureaucratic-speak by one of our arch-pragmatists, that the avant-garde is now so institutionally entrenched that, more than ever, we need to tap out a different drumbeat. We need an art which works its material into idiomatic vision. An art which meets mechanical reproduction with animating metaphysical import. An art that mounts the steps, ready to unpick the Zeitgeist.

And as far as protests went, I was ready for more, to fail again, and each time to fail better.

Introduction

Who is this middle-aged man? (see Plate 7). He has a long lean face and holds a warning finger against his thin lips. *Be silent*, he seems to say, *be minimal in all that you do*. Underneath the photograph there is a quotation from his writing: 'there is no solution because there is no problem'.[1] It is a picture of Marcel Duchamp, the first conceptualist.

We are not as familiar with his work or his image as we are with that of Picasso's, yet it is now turning out that his influence may be greater than that of the maestro. Indeed, it could convincingly be claimed that if the exuberant Picasso ruled the first half of the twentieth century, the lean minimalist Duchamp has ruled the second half. For behind most of the work gathered in the last cerebral rooms of our self-preening Museums of Modern Art there lurks the silent influence of Duchamp with his thin finger at his closed lips. As early as 1969 the artist Joseph Kosuth was to claim: 'all art (after Duchamp) is conceptual (in nature) because art only exists conceptually'.[2]

This is only to note the dominant prevailing fashion in the visual arts, the systematic flight from the aesthetic and the imaginative over the last three or four decades. Here it is pertinent to remember that the philosopher Hegel was convinced that art had reached a final state of irrecoverable depletion at the beginning of the nineteenth century and would never again recover. 'Art', he wrote, 'no longer affords that satisfaction of spiritual want which earlier epochs and peoples have sought therein and have found therein . . . the beautiful days of Greek art and the golden time of the late middle ages are gone by.'[3] He went on to state that the abstract, speculative and scientific nature of his own time conspired against any further artistic renaissance. These remain haunting words at the beginning of the twenty-first century when Hegel's notion of the end of history has, again, returned as a mesmerizing hypothesis.

In the dark light of Duchamp's work and influence we might be tempted to call Hegel a remarkable prophet but, of course, it is not as simple as that. Much great art has been created since the death of Hegel, especially in the art form of film, a radical new medium for representing the images and narratives of life which the philosopher could not have possibly anticipated. And then, contra Hegel, art does not have to be historically sanctioned. It can be oppositional. It does not have to be of its time. Its creation can be antithetical to the age. From this perspective, art should seek to express those elements of life – often metaphysical and poetic – which have been repressed or maligned under the reign of technology and the many impersonal forces of human alienation. Such subverting art does not seek to reproduce the prevailing state of attenuated consciousness but, rather, to keep open delicate states of being and apprehension which are in danger of being wiped out. Its function here is, at once, visionary and remedial.

Such art exists, we might say, for the sake of alterity. Significant remedial art *in* our time – wherever it is infrequently created and infrequently found, not often in the major galleries of London, Paris and New York – does not have to be *of* our time. For it could be there to express an act of creative maladjustment, an act of resistance, an awkward but quite essential otherness to the technological age and its dominant mode of consciousness. Its very absence from newspaper columns and TV chat shows could thus become a vital sign, but in no way a definitive proof, of its aesthetic power and primordial vitality.

This is to begin to define the need for a kind of metaphysical art – metaphysical in its cast and orientation but not, as I have argued throughout this book, in any prescribed agenda of doctrinal beliefs or values. The more the Zeitgeist (following, in this case, the example of Marcel Duchamp) insists on the redundancy of expressive and imaginative art, the more it may paradoxically need it. At the moment, the avant-garde has become the privileged Establishment. Its work is comfortably housed in national institutions, bank vaults and art colleges and hailed by bankers, journalists, bishops, critics, curators and passing crackpots. By a curious irony the subversive anti-art concepts of Duchamp now thrive as artistic orthodoxy. They have congealed into a deadly tradition, a tame absurdity, a predictable iconoclasm housed in the Tate Gallery and acclaimed by colour supplements and academics, which threatens nothing and no-one – except, of course, through their collective tyranny, the very life of the spirit and the elusive quick of creative consciousness.

What, exactly, is wrong with the notion of conceptual art?

First, there is a matter of definition. How can one have a coherent movement called conceptual art? Conceptual thinking is the task of philosophy and other forms of discursive linguistic enquiry. Sensuous thinking – in febrile relation to the imagination – is the distinctive task of the artist. His or her thinking is done through a continuous engagement with the expressive medium of the art. Artists transform the glorious material of paint into embodied vision. This is what Matisse meant when he said that a painter's thought could never be separated from his pictorial means. Conceptual art, we could say, is bad philosophy – for its use of language is extremely limited, but it is also depleted art, for there is virtually no personal handling of the material. The physical work with the medium being entirely minimal the artistic form is, thereby, radically maimed.

Second, conceptual art tends to elevate to the point of bathos the status of found objects. Here the most insightful and witty comment has been made by the contemporary poet, John Heath-Stubbs:

> Bunch was an unremarkable dog
> Till to everyone's surprize
> The shit he left on the carpet
> Won the Turner Prize.[4]

If, as Nicholas Serota has argued in line with many sociological art critics, any object in an art gallery with a title or a placard **DO NOT TOUCH THIS IS A WORK OF ART** is thereby a work of art, then there can be no intrinsic meaning to art and no criteria for its aesthetic evaluation. Under this sociological rule, art becomes little more than a social phenomenon in a prescribed setting (a gallery) to be talked about. This is a conception much loved by the mass media and the late-night chat shows – ever seeking the easy clichés of the sensational instant – but it is not a conception which enhances or illuminates the art form. It is entirely in keeping that journalists have become powerful players in the creation of reputations and movements. As early as 1968 the art critic Herbert Read warned his readers of movements that were not artistically coherent but 'the creation of journalists anxious to find a label for phenomena they do not understand'.[5]

Tellingly, when Damian Hirst won the Turner Prize in 1995, the art journalist William Feaver claimed that he deserved it for his effrontery. Under the inane headline HIRST COMES FIRST he wrote: 'Damien Hirst got the prize for panache and effrontery, and for livening things up by gracing them with impact in, yes, formaldehyde.'[6] He then went on to write: 'Hirst is not a curator's favourite . . . and yet he has this immense global pull. He uses fame as others use solvents.'[7] But since when has panache and effrontery, fame and global pull (whatever that means) been aesthetic criteria for the evaluation of art? They could equally well describe the antics of the French Fascist Le Pen or the South American footballer Maradona. As concepts they are impotent to point to intrinsic artistic significance. They are little more than media tags, hot head-lines, for a consumer mass-society. But if effrontery and panache are turned by jaded cosmopolitan journalists into criteria for judging art, then how can one stop Bounce's shit getting into the Tate Gallery? And once Bounce's excrement is there how can any one stop the academic sociologists entering and earnestly explaining that because the shit is located there – and not Marks and Spencer or McDonald's – it must merit the word art, for art is simply what you find displayed in art galleries?

Third, conceptual artists, extending and professionalizing the work of Duchamp, have (like Damian Hirst) come to depend on an array of technicians for the construction of their work. This means that there is an inevitable loss of personal idiom. All the work comes to possess a technician's mechanical impersonality. The synthetic finish negates that human style which traditionally has been the artistic culmination of personal struggle and aesthetic labour. Such impersonality spells the death of art as idiomatic expression and ushers in the insolent reign of the mechanical. Of course, it is true that a synthetic finish reflects our synthetic age, but, again, can that be a sufficient quality to make it significant art? According to one authority on Marcel Duchamp:

> Duchamp recognized that the art object will have a different presence in a world where its function is no longer 'religious, philosophical, moral', and that, in an age of facile mechanical reproduction, it will take its value from something other than mimesis in the traditional sense.[8]

But the question remains: if art-makers merely reproduce work mechanically, what can they bring to the world of mass production which does not already exist in the society at large? To put the point more bluntly: what is the point of reproducing the impersonal dehumanized status quo? A Coca-Cola bottle on a stand. A beefburger inflated to ten times its size. A rectangle of bricks. If this is its degraded mimetic function, then, perhaps, Hegel was right: art is over. In which case conceptual work heralds not a new beginning but the bathetic end, a vacuous epitaph.

Another distorting fallacy in much contemporary art is the notion that art exists primarily to trigger language. The art object – as it is impersonally called – would seem to exist merely to provoke any kind of linguistic thought. For this reason there is very little to be *seen* in conceptual art. It doesn't engage the eye: indeed, the more one looks the less one sees. Conceptual art is, it would seem, no more than the sum total of all that can be *formulated* about it. It is a language game on the edge of arbitrary babble, loved by the media and the pundits, but in truth badly betraying the eye and the imagination and depriving us of what, in the hidden interior world of being, we most need – an opportunity to contemplate those forms of metaphysical significance that live on the other side of our numbed and narrowed consciousness.

Yet the more banal and vacuous the dominant art becomes, the more there grows at the same time an all but inexpressible yearning for the deep imaginative art it has all but destroyed. Out of the boredom there emerges a passion for the excluded element. Discriminating individuals begin to look again for an art dedicated to meaning through the sensuous transformations of the materials used. They search for artists whose work invites profound acts of aesthetic contemplation – in brief, they seek out the antithesis of conceptualism and the creative answer to it. I want now to look at four contemporary art-makers in the light of these remarks: the painters Andrzej Jackowski, Harold Mockford and Mary Lloyd Jones and the sculptor John Meirion Morris. They may not be great artists, but I want to suggest that they are *significant* artists – representing many other unacknowledged artists across Europe and around the world – revealing through the aesthetic power of their chosen medium dimensions of experience essential to our diminished humanity. They are artists in search of what cannot be mechanically reproduced. Their work exists to transcend the facile status quo and to embody the forms of alterity.

The sparse lyrical work of Andrzej Jackowski

For some years now Andrzej Jackowski has been concerned to articulate through his paintings the inner life of reverie and its own associative logic. His work moves somewhere between dreaming and waking. As a young painter finding his way for years he drew only with his left hand so as to break the spell of natural representation. His truth is imaginative truth to the inner world and to those elected objects which carry its poetic language. His most powerful images derive from the deep cellars of the human memory, either his own personal memory of a precarious childhood or the collective memory of the human race. The paintings are particularly powerful when the two sources of imagery merge and we find ourselves standing awe-struck before a vast image which is both deeply personal and yet also archetypal.

In the foreground of one painting titled *The Vigilant* (1984) (Plate 8) a vast head floats on the tide; behind it there is a small boat in which a man is carrying a roll of canvas: behind the boat is a stormy and turbulent sky. The particular and compelling cluster of images carry with them deep resonances – historical and archetypal – concerning annihilation and redemption, work and reparation. Indeed the latter seems extremely important in the work of Jackowski. The signs and artefacts of labour – pots, tools, ladders, fences, walls, chairs, tables – litter his canvases. It is as if we are the sum total of what we have made or struggled to make and that what has been made is always at risk, always threatened by the erosions and erasures of time, the cosmic indifference of nature and the destructive energies of the human mind itself. His early work, in particular, depicts precarious settlements. Significantly, many of the painter's most shocking images derive from the Holocaust.

The dominant note of a Jackowski painting is dense and sombre. His work moves across a somewhat limited but convincing spectrum from freezing trauma to quiet expectancy. The extreme ends of this feeling spectrum are marked by two fine paintings. One is called *Toxic Tank* (1996); the other *The Boy who Broke the Spell* (1996) (Plates 9 and 10). They merit close attention.

In both paintings, in a characteristic metaphysical leap, an ordinary table becomes a sacred altar – a holy site of possible sacrifice and possible transformation. In Jackowski's world of engaged reverie the most ordinary object – a shoe, a discarded toy, an insect, a case, a wardrobe, a bed – can become a most extra-ordinary carrier, bearing some universal portion of human life. Thus, again and again, in his recent work the simple everyday table becomes a terrible altar for a variety of possible transmutations.

In *Toxic Tank* the table is white and functional. On it stands the tank with a blood-red lid. Inside the tank there is the suggestion of moving fish but at the bottom lies a bloody fish-like body (is there a reference here to the 'fish' Christ?) or, possibly, a raw aborted foetus. At one side of the table stands the white 'priest'. He is faceless. He is the expert, the bureaucrat, the nameless one, the one who performs but has no idea what he does. Where his heart should be there hangs a cold stone-like object. But the most dreadful element in this most disturbing painting is the shocking pink daubed with blood-coloured strokes which forms not so much a background as the dimension of feeling in which the unredeemed and unredeemable objects stand. *Toxic Tank* is a version of the Holocaust, and contemplating it we become its appalled and implicated witnesses.

In dialectical contrast *The Boy who Broke the Spell* is permeated with an expectant light and has a serrated green-brown 'background'. In this painting the table is red and has a pink cloth laid over it. On its surface there lies a long thin box, a greyish coffin. Lying inside, only partly visible, is the figure of a young boy. He could be dead. He could be sleeping. He could be waiting. He could, certainly, be dreaming.

Near the boy's feet on the table is a jam jar with some flowering twigs and near the jar is a single red shoe. The table casts a darkish shadow on the sombre brown floor. Against one of the bright red legs of the table there rises a spiky plant which breaks into a subdued orange flame. The painting expresses a sense of expectancy, of possible resurrection. It expresses the feeling of Holy Saturday suspended between the unspeakable Good Friday and the joyous Easter Sunday. It is *almost* celebratory and is the antithesis of *Toxic Tank*. Placed together they work dialectically, giving us compelling images of the contrary states of human consciousness. They are restrained examples of the contemporary metaphysical imagination.

Andrzej Jackowski is neither comfortable, nor fashionable, but he is a significant painter. His best work matters. He has evolved his own distinctive style to depict the stations of our being. In the most powerful of his metaphors he discloses immense anguish, the fear of disfigurement, the prospect of annihilation. But he also offers redemptive moments, the moods and modes of atonement, the place of hope, the power of expectancy. If by metaphysical art we denote that art which re-describes and re-positions the objects of our daily phenomenal world so that they become the metaphors of our own predicament then it would seem essential to include him in any list of contemporary metaphysical painters.

We may not be a problem in need of a solution, as Duchamp claimed; but we are a predicament in need of metaphors so that we can see who we are and who we might be a little more clearly. Andrzej Jackowski's austere work adds to our stock of metaphors and in a world of postmodern exhaustion still has the power to release afresh our feeling life.

Art with an encompassing vision: the work of Mary Lloyd Jones

Mary Lloyd Jones is a painter who addresses our feeling life but in a very different manner. She paints with a greater exuberance, with a greater elan and spontaneity. Her work is a form of modern landscape painting, celebrating in a semi-abstract mode the spirit of place. And she draws on very different traditions from Andrzej Jackowski.

Until recently Mary Lloyd Jones worked in Aberbanc in the heart of rural Wales. She settled there in 1975, turning a traditional primary school into a vast studio area. She worked in that remote village with a single-minded tenacity, committed not only to her own evolving work but also to the regeneration of art in Wales. Her own background was Welsh and Welsh-speaking; it was also deeply rural. She was born in 1934 in Pontarfynach (Devil's Bridge) about twelve miles east of Aberystwyth, where she went to school. In 1951 she went on to Cardiff Art College.

Being an artist in any place is not easy. Being an artist in Wales can seem like a contradiction in terms, for the expressive energies of the Welsh culture, for a complex variety of reasons, rushed almost entirely into the language of poetry and rhetoric leaving the other arts, especially the visual, neglected and misunderstood. For a number of years Mary Lloyd Jones clearly suffered a sense of isolation, an acute feeling of exile in her own culture. How could one become a painter in Wales where there was no sustained visual arts tradition?

Of course, like earlier Romantics, one could turn for inspiration to the great and ancient mountains of Wales, but Mary Lloyd Jones discovered something else, something more intimate, something much closer to home. She was given a quilt (Plate 11) made by her great grandmother. Here was a visual artefact made by her own class, her own people, her own family. It was clearly functional but it was also clearly beautiful. One had only to lift it off the bed and hang it on the wall to grasp the compelling symmetry of its form. It was, at the same moment, art and craft. It was both public and intimate – belonging, as it did, to the obvious daily needs of a living culture. For the artist it was a revelation. The quilt was not only a family memento, but also a fierce manifesto. It proclaimed three things – art belongs where we live and work, it is committed to beauty, it can be made by women.

In the 1970s Mary Lloyd Jones sought consciously to extend the tradition that was historically hers. She engaged with fabrics and with the labour traditionally associated with women – with washing, sewing, dyeing. But the themes of her work expanded to embrace the drama of natural landscape, the magical markings of ancestors and the power of ancient cave paintings. These batiks show recognizable landscapes, but landscapes indelibly marked by the struggles and aspirations of human consciousness. The quilt tradition was being acknowledged, extended and transformed. Its influence can be detected, if more indirectly, in the paintings, particularly the water colours. Here some of the standard geometrical figures of the quilt composition can be witnessed (but with new spiritual resonances in play) as also the clear patches of colour placed adroitly side by side to make the pattern of the picture.

But Mary Lloyd Jones' work also belongs unequivocally to a central European movement which we could term *spiritual expressionism*. It is a strong gestural tradition in the visual arts where the final vision of the painting is discovered in the engaged physical handling of the very stuff of paint. In this school much of the painter's meaning is apprehended in the startlingly fresh textures and transformations of the labile material – simply, paint in all its volatility – as it is applied to the canvas or paper. In this tradition one would have to place Rembrandt who adored the moist, shining, palpable *substance* of paint – but also the twentieth-century painters: Nolde, Bomberg and Hitchens. At its most radical this tradition creates a kind of symphonic painting where the colours and tones, working simultaneously, create a powerful mood through which the meaning of the spirit is articulated and the ineffable given sudden unexpected accommodation. Bomberg talked famously of 'the spirit in the mass'. The analogue is with music – though unlike music the marks still often retain a reference to a recognizable physical world which they seek to interpret – and the method that of the most urgent intuition. Tellingly, these painters have exerted a seminal influence on the work of Mary Lloyd Jones.

She invariably works with great rapidity, allowing her spontaneous quick-moving intuitions to determine the urgent flow of paint and to resolve its unexpected meetings and chance collisions at top speed. *Carpe diem!* At best, the result is a painting which has an irrepressible freshness – rather as one might imagine in myth the perception of God on the first day of Creation. Often looking at her work we feel we are looking down from a great height. We see an aerial view. Perspective (that tedious art of calculation) yields here to simultaneous vision and the experience of Paradise – for we are not looking *at* but rather participating *in* what we see. All is immediate flow. The landscape a river of colour.

Much of the artist's work is celebratory and exerts an instant magic. And yet it is not always as unambiguous as that – for many of the Welsh landscapes depict the Rheidol Valley with its ground scarred by the disused lead mines and disfigured by the colonial angular planting of countless conifers. In some of these fine paintings a savage anger dismembers the natural forms and an inchoate rage splatters the canvas. (see, for example, *Cwm Rheidol (Scars)*, Plate 12). And yet, even so, there are points of redemption. For example, in some of the turbulent Rheidol Valley paintings, an ancient mystical language will half insert itself or a divine geometry – often, the sacred triangle – emerge to complement the turbulent flux. The unnatural wounds of the landscape, the deep industrial scars, the old derelict castles are there, but even as they appear they suggest something infinitely more, an even older order that lies beyond them and before them. For the paintings are deeply polysemic and, unlike the pessimistic poetry of R. S. Thomas, fundamentally affirmative of life, at least when it is lived in a connected web of relationship, ecological, human and sacred.

This brings me to the third great force working in and through the paintings. The more one considers and contemplates the work, the more one becomes aware of a spiritual visual language. Her landscape is not 'an environment' – that ugly word showing our mechanical distance from Nature – but more like a shrine of the Goddess. One of her works – dated 1988 – is actually called *Barclodiad y Gawres (The Goddess with an Apron-full)* (Plate 13). The many marks that congregate at unexpected points in the landscapes are not doodles or the arbitrary deposits of idle fantasy, but the dramatic marks of the missing Goddess, her ancient signs and signatures. The zig-zag lines, the serpentine curves, the spiralling shapes, the dark triangles – all invoke the absence of the female God. This is her old visual language. The lines are not casual for they repeat and extend the very marks made in palaeolithic and neolithic times on rocks and stones and tombs, in the open air as, also, in the darkness of the caves. These markings, which compose an iconography in their own right, have been collected and interpreted in Marija Gimbutas' book *The Language of the Goddess* – a book which has inspired Mary Lloyd Jones and been a formative influence on her late work.

The conscious resuscitation of the bardic alphabet of Iolo Morganwg and the ancient Irish Ogam serve a similar purpose. The bold geometrical letters move like dark presences across some of the landscapes as if to reclaim an earlier and broken contract. Here the aim of the painting is to reassert for modern times a lost connection, at once sacred and ecological. This, surely, is a clear and courageous answer to the exhausted avant-gardes of the metropolis.

No artist works entirely alone – and if she did, then no-one would understand her. The artist always stands inside history and culture. There is no alternative. But the aim of the artist is not to mechanically reproduce the synthetic world which surrounds him. That is the route to anasthesia, a *numbing* down. The aim is more challenging: it is dialectical engagement and cultural transformation in our own time, in our own place, in our own idiom. At best, this inward revision creates further common vision, a compelling sense of meaning and possibility. At first, this is experienced as a sense of startled recognition, a quiver of intellectual joy, a spiritual *yes*. And then a fuller understanding comes gradually in its wake. This is the case with nearly all forms of aesthetic appreciation.

The poet-philosopher, Nietzsche, in his *The Will to Power* wrote: 'What does a pessimistic art signify? Is it not a *contradiction*? – Yes.'[9] The late twentieth century, after the first high period of modernism, has been marked not only by pessimistic art, but by an art which delights only in panache and effrontery, in a breezy nihilism. Like Andrzej Jackowski, Mary Lloyd Jones' work marks a way forward. She has discovered the elements of an ecological understanding and a powerful way of representing it.

The visionary work of Harold Mockford

Like Andrzej Jackowski and Mary Lloyd Jones, the painter Harold Mockford lives at the far side of fashion and the daily manufacture of instant reputations. He is, at once, a quiet visionary and a determined outsider. For him art is the necessary expressive means of rendering his own spiritual apprehension of the world. He has lived all his life in Sussex and after some preliminary training at Eastbourne College of Art has educated himself, avoiding schools and artistic mafias, so as to keep faith with his developing vision. His isolation and independence has kept his handling of paint agile, personal and deeply poetic. But it would be wrong to conclude that while Mockford's vision appears naive that he is a naive painter. Far from it. His work testifies to a number of deeply sublimated influences: Samuel Palmer, Van Gogh, Pierre Bonnard, Carel Weight, Mark Rothko. The diverse influences have been finely assimilated into a style that has enabled Mockford to convert the Sussex landscape and seascape into the most compelling images of magical transformation. Not unlike the isolated William Blake, Harold Mockford has nominated his own tradition to create his own distinctive mythology.

Anyone familiar with East Sussex in England will have no trouble identifying the immediate physical locations which are the sources of most of his paintings. Again and again, in his direct dramatic canvasses one recognizes the actual site: the Long Man of Wilmington, Firle Beacon, Birling Gap, Beachy Head, Eastbourne Pier and Belle Tout Lighthouse and Newhaven Harbour (see *Night Ferry* (1999), Plate 14). And even if one doesn't know the exact place, one immediately registers the feminine undulations of the Downs, the slender church spire rising above a clump of trees, the small gates, the long stone walls, the disappearing chalk paths and the treeless uninterrupted horizons. One could draw a fifteen mile circle around Eastbourne and have immediate ownership of Mockford's landscape. This is where the artist was born. This is where he has lived his life. At one level his work is an epithany in paint to the small patch of nature and culture he was born into and, no doubt, many of the chosen sites are resonant with childhood memory. What we have then in his extensive work is a wonderful local affirmation. Yet to see Mockford primarily as a painter of landscape is to badly misconstrue his work and to limit its true value.

Yes, of course, we recognize the place in the painting – and the title of the work often simply names it. But we see something else as well – a unique poetic transformation. An art of alchemy. In this transformation the *recognizable* outer object becomes simultaneously the ambiguous vessel of inner meaning. The transposition of literal colour into imaginative colour is indicative. In Mockford the English grey sky can often hang down in veils of red and orange, the fields stretch across the canvas in an unfamiliar dark ochre, the sheep and horses can stand in unapologetic blue and the white chalk cliffs rise into a cloudy green. But the poetic choice of colour is not an isolated event – it is merely part of an entire transposition of nature into another spiritual key. Working always from memory, Mockford consistently dramatizes his immediate perceptions, tends to add narrative elements, finds or invents small moments of radiance – a wave breaking white near the cliffs, sunlight hitting the corner of a field or a remote patch of water – and converts the local into the universal.

Quite often in his work there is a sense of impending drama – as if one stood at the edge of an imminent apocalypse or some *moment* of spiritual revelation or simply near a small gate which, if opened, would lead into a childhood paradise where everything is complete and the smallest object bright with its own significance. In fact, the free-standing country gate – both taking us into and cutting us off from the ground on the other side – is a key Mockford emblem and an excellent example of how a quite ordinary object is converted into a symbol of the human spirit. The outer geography carries the inner landscape of the soul. The paintings greet us like events which are about to take place. They are not conceptions but mysteries about to unfold – if we can only learn to live aesthetically inside them.

For example, take the painting *Waiting to go* (Plate 15). The more we look at it the more we feel caught up in a dramatic but not quite resolved moment. The sky shifts through three colours – dark rust, orange, pale ochre – not unlike a Rothko painting except that at the centre float two naive clouds taking us away from pure abstraction and locating us in a magical figurative world. Mockford is keen to keep us in a world of representation, but it is a world of magical re-description rather than simple denotation. He is, as I have implied, the master of dramatic imagination. Under the clouds and to the left we notice the ferry boat returning to Newhaven from Dieppe. As our eyes drop to the foreground of the painting we notice the parked cars, the brown fences and the buildings above which on the sagging telegraph wires the swifts and swallows gather ready to migrate. Then, finally, beneath these congregating birds one notices three tiny figures standing at a gate which would appear to open straight into the sea. Two of the figures stand close to each other – a man and a woman; the third figure – a woman – stands slightly apart. Here are all the elements of a small human drama over which the sky stands like a biblical revelation. The painting is animated by a half-resolved tension set up by the three dramatic levels of land, sea and sky, by the suggestion of imminent return and the imminent departure and also by the three figures standing against the gate. The colours are full of expectancy. A heightened moment of being stands suspended before us.

Not all of Mockford's paintings fit the pattern I have described. There is an austere sequence of autobiographical paintings which stand apart. These paintings are courageous visual explorations of inner unease and dislocation. They represent the dark side of the artist's creativity. In one of the paintings, *The Ancestors* (1993) (Plate 16), the artist stands to attention in the foreground. The frame cuts off his head as he stares away from the viewer as well as from his father who sits on the other side of the picture in the background. Behind him on the wall is an image of his grandparents. Three generations are brought together in the same small room. The father and grandparents stand together, comfortable, at ease with the continuity; while the painter stands apart, staring across the flow of time and connection. He stands to attention, outwardly compliant and inwardly disconnected. The mirror over the fireplace which physically divides the son from his father and grandfather is blank. A stark and powerful image of alienation – the very antithesis to the lyrical celebrations of landscape and inscape of his dominant work.

Harold Mockford describes his paintings as acts of discovery. The day I met him he was working on a painting based on a woman he has seen feeding some wild birds in Seaford. This movement of observation, he explains, was a heightened moment of perception. It is the starting point of the new work. But as he works on the image it moves more and more into metaphor. It accumulates further meaning. The woman comes to symbolize a portion of being, in particular, a living concern with the natural order. As the painting evolves, Mockford explains, he will add new elements of story. This, he insists, will further change the original vision and keep it vital. Then when the painting has reached a certain telling moment of strangeness he will leave it and turn to the next composition. The painting does not reach a formal perfection but, rather, a point of mystery which can be taken no further. Everything he says confirms that his paintings are, at root, dramatic metaphors of the soul held up for our contemplation, physical and metaphysical, local and universal at the same movement.

In his book of collected reviews and short essays, *Testimonies*, Michael Hamburger characterizes poetry as being both anachronistic and utopian. It is anachronistic, he argues, because at its deepest level poetry works outside time. It is Utopian because, beyond whatever its immediate personal and geographic context, it is always both nowhere and everywhere – forever present. Mockford's paintings have the same powerful virtues. His best work tangibly demonstrates the union of art and spirit and points us way beyond the world of instant reputation and mesmerizing fashion. Not abstract concepts, but embodied revelations. Only one who has kept himself apart from the tyranny of fashion could have painted them.

The mythological sculpture of John Meirion Morris

In a review of John Meirion Morris' work the art critic Shelagh Hourahane wrote:

> John Meirion Morris claims the difficult ground of spirituality, meditation and contemplation with an absolute certainty and a powerful presence. He also treads the twisting paths of celtic ancestry, reaching back in time and imagination to contact the emotive and elusive past.[10]

This begins to point to the somewhat startling character of John Meirion Morris's sculptural works; it points both to their inner authority and to their major inspirational source in early Celtic art and design – a debt which makes his work dramatically different in feel and idiom from the images of Mockford, Lloyd Jones and Jackowski.

Yet, without question, his work also belongs to the unacknowledged spiritual tradition of the twentieth century – particularly to the sculptural tradition of Moore, Brancusi and Epstein. He shares with Epstein a gift to create both powerful representational figures and work which is essentially primordial in nature. It is the latter work which concerns me here. Something of the scope of this archetypal work is brought out well by Epstein in his *Autobiography* where he wrote of Indian sculpture:

> In Indian work of this nature there is a deeply religious element, sometimes amounting to a fury of passion which is elemental in its power. Shiva dances, creating the world and destroying it, his large rhythms conjure up vast aeons of time, and his movements have a relentless and magical power of incantation . . . The modern sculpture without religion, without direction, tradition and stability, is at a terrible disadvantage compared with the sculptors of previous periods.[11]

The work being advocated here has nothing to do with the representation of actual individuals or the literal world, but with the fundamental elements of life – sex, birth, death, transformation, eternity – symbolized in expressive forms which are compelling to the human imagination. In this great primordial tradition art is never for the sake of art but for the sake of the spirit and the enhancement of individual and communal life. Art is not a formal 'aesthetic' or a publicity stunt but a transformative activity.

Describing his own approach John Meirion Morris has written:

> Sculpture for me is a kind of meditation. I meditate on images which enter my imagination, in other words I respond instinctively to them and develop them whether they be images of protest or mythical or religious images. One experience which forms an essential part of the mythological/religious images is the traumatic experience of life and death. I find that the experience of death, or inner release, forms an intrinsic part of the rhythm of life, the creative process and religious experience. While meditating I feel instinctively that I am getting in touch with something basic and religious which is part of our essence as beings and part of nature.[12]

These *images* might best be conceived as archetypal in nature, images, that is to say, which are the a priori imaginal correlates of our diverse instincts. Yet their actual expression is always inside a specific culture and it is here that we encounter the other essential aspect of John Meirion Morris's work. It is profoundly traditional. It is Celtic in rhythm and organization and deeply influenced by the La Téne period of Celtic Art. The sculptor himself has made a sustained study of this period in terms of its spiritual understanding. If the images appear to arise spontaneously in meditation they are yet shaped by a tradition which lies at the root of his own culture. The very urgent and the very ancient come together and are, often, further extended into Welsh culture by references (in most of the titles) to the literary masterpiece of *The Mabinogion*. What we are describing, then, is an archetypal art which has one deep root in the natural energies of the human mind–body and another deep root penetrating far down into the cultural deposits of La Téne art (500 BC–AD 200) and even further back, into the prehistorical. At its best, the fusion is as remarkable as it is complete and utterly unselfconscious.

Morris's sculpture demands a particular kind of attention. It breaks with both the classical tradition and the dominant European tradition in sculpture. In looking at a work by John Meirion Morris we are not invited to move *around* the work, to move from one aesthetic sensation to another, to cumulatively build up the whole; rather, we are frequently confronted by a single gaze which would have us be still and would transfix us by its power. The gaze would freeze us in our tracks and make us not restless explorers of the aesthetic but spellbound contemplators of some elemental truth. Take *Modron* (1996), for example (Plate 17). The work directly confronts us. The only visual movement allowed is a vertical movement up and down the length of the long body. If the impersonal wisdom of the face (framed by the leaf-like emanations of nature) first arrests us, then our gaze, held in by the two uplifted arms, is only free to follow the line of the elongated neck down to the womb (where there is embryonic life) and then further down to the base of the figure where stretches a fallen corpse-like figure. The only movement then left by the fierce symmetry of the icon (for icon it most certainly is) is the return journey upwards through birth to the serene contemplative consciousness of the head. The narrative of the sculpture operates solely through the vertical axis and its meaning is clearly metaphysical. Enlightenment, it declares, comes out of the affirmative recognition of birth and death. If birth is the thesis and death the antithesis, then the synthesis lies in an understanding which transcends both and creates the third term of spiritual understanding. At the same time as the figure represents the all-inclusive goddess, it simultaneously embodies the deciduous Tree of Life: buds, leaves, calyxes, branches are active throughout the work. The act of contemplation takes place within the biological world. There is no Cartesian or Christian dualism here. The spiritual exists within the matrix of nature. Mind and body are different aspects of the same driving energy.

Modron, then, is the archetypal goddess image but its formulation remains distinctively Celtic. In fact, it is a contemporary version of an ancient artefact, namely the relief from Tal-y-llyn in Gwynedd circa 100 BC. Here we find a metaphysical ideogram which substantially informs the structure of *Modron* and provides the tradition through which it is to be understood. If the relief from Tal-y-llyn is a kind of spiritual diagram, relating to birth, death and transformation, then *Modron* is its contemporary sculptural and artistic realization. There are other allusions in *Modron*, too. The enfolded head has a striking resemblance to a number of La Téne heads (to the stone head from Heidelberg *c*. 450 BC, for example) while the creature of death at the base of *Modron* resembles the upside-down creature under the Great Mother on the Gundelstrup Cauldron (Denmark, *c*.250 BC). As with early Celtic art, John Meirion Morris' work is highly symmetrical. This is particularly true of *Modron*, where if one were to split the image down the middle, one would be left with two virtually identical parts.

Again, the symmetry of *Bran* (1993) – a symbolic bird which directly confronts us with its male and female oppositions – has an almost mathematical rigour (see Plate 18). On either side the piece advances upwards from *three* wing pieces, to *two* dragon's tongues, to *one* elongated crying head. Similarly, as if to emphasize the spiritual element, the elongated neck and head (the top half) is smooth while the bottom half (linked to nature and femininity and death) is rough, textured, elaborate. Once again, one is reminded of a metaphysics which envisages consciousness rising up through the manifold of nature (and sexuality) to give expression to its essential spiritual meaning. At the same time the bird is also Welsh (its dragon's tongues are unmistakable) and symbolizes, at another level, the plight of a culture which faces extinction. The scream is the cry of anguish before such a prospect. The mythological bird can carry febrile political messages and more effectively for their being part of a greater system of meaning and allusion.

It is often thought that Celtic art is ornamental; in a sense it is, but this tendency towards repetition and complex elaboration does not mark an aesthetic doodling so much as a rhythmic way of thinking, a kinaesthetic route to wisdom. In her book *Pagan Celtic Britain* Anne Ross writes about the number three:

> For the Celts, three was a significant number, having a magico-religious connotation. The early Irish tales contain references to three semi-divine heroes rather than one, born at a single birth and being given the same name, but distinguishing epithets; deities are grouped in threes; the traditional lore of both Wales and Ireland is preserved in a series of triadic statements, and this predilection for the number three can be discerned throughout the Celtic tradition.[13]

The significance of three, indeed, relates to the major theme of our interpretation: birth, death, and its transcendence. In the work of John Meirion Morris many of the sculptures, following this metaphysical triad, can be seen to divide into life (often just below the centre of the piece), the underworld (at the base) and the exalted triumph of cosmic consciousness (rising through the top half of the work to be finally expressed in the eyes and forehead of the work). This triadic structure corresponds exactly with the figure of *Modron*. We find here a visual grammar which has a profound reference to the spiritual world, a syntax of sacred sense.

Most recently John Meirion Morris has turned to the role of public monumental sculpture. His *Trywerin* (1997) – Plates 19 and 20 – is another symbolic bird designed to stand 28 feet high above the side of Trywerin reservoir where a Welsh village was flooded to provide water for Liverpool in the 1960s. The icon is a powerful protest against cultural and material exploitation and an assertion of the freedom and power of the Celtic spirit. The bird's beak, as in *Bran*, rises into the higher dimension of consciousness while the great splayed wings bear within them (see Plate 20) a chorus of shrieking and outraged heads sounding their lament for an exploited nation. John Meirion Morris has explained: 'I believe it is the role of sculpture to make people aware of their identity, their cultural roots. Without roots, without identity, one cannot fly.'[14] Here, again, one finds an expression of the artist as a spiritual and cultural mediator, making public truths that are in constant danger of being forgotten.

This is engaged public sculpture. It labours on behalf of collective memory and on behalf of the threatened community. The work urges a greater understanding and the play of informed consciousness. It would have us connect with a great historic past and with energies that lie submerged there. It would have us see ourselves, not as acquisitive consumers, *but as threatened historic animals with visionary propensities.*

The *Trywerin* sculpture is not ironic, not parodic, not post-modernist but I would suggest, without doubt, the work *is* revolutionary. Like the headless torso of Apollo, as experienced by the poet Rilke, it would have us change our lives. It is the very stuff of personal and social transformation.

If Epstein lamented the position of the modern sculptor without religion, direction or tradition, here, at least, is one living sculptor in Wales who (like Mary Lloyd Jones) has located his ancestors and put their vision and their artistic formulations to further creative use, to remind us of all but lost spiritual and political possibilities.

Conclusion

We are living through an unprecedented crisis in the history of the visual arts. It is a crisis of representation and meaning. The case against the various avant-gardes of the last century can now be presented with a philosophical cogency which has still to be recognized. Quite simply, the visual arts have too often failed to represent and aesthetically embody the full range and the peculiar depth of the human spirit. They have failed to connect with the historic past. And they have failed to find an audience beyond a tiny, faddish, media-centred minority. Instead of addressing and liberating the imagination much modern and contemporary art has merely added to the symptoms of decay, loss and futility. As we begin the third millennium we are in need of a more fundamental imaginative orientation; a deeper historical, spiritual and eco-logical reconnection.

The artists I have glanced at in this chapter may not be *great* painters (time alone will tell) but they are *significant* painters working against the flow; they each express a vision of life in their own idiomatic styles; they each work their media with both love and skill; they each work a tradition and build on it, a tradition which in the case of Mary Lloyd Jones and John Meirion Morris goes back into the dark prehistorical consciousness of life; they, thus, connect us to an encompassing world and add to our sense of being here. There is neither effrontery nor panache to be found in their work, neither minimal irony nor 'global pull', but there *is* a profound sense of a continuous artistic struggle to address the imagination and to keep the ineffable spirit of life both (paradoxically) grounded and labile. They are manifestations of a poetics of culture dedicated to the understanding and enhancement of life.

Coda

The thoughts expressed in this book are neither easy nor comfortable. Yet the depleted state of our education and culture call for the excavation of critical concepts and subversive metaphors which are in danger of being lost under the glittering debris of consumer products and the leaden piles of bureaucratic missives. These concepts and metaphors speak to our condition as ethical, aesthetic and metaphysical animals. To deny their importance is, somehow, to make us less than we potentially are, is to demean and diminish us, is, finally, to brutalize us.

At the same time they are not there to be assimilated as consumer options, as alternative lifestyles. They demand our open presence, our critical engagement, our living spirit. I hope I have managed to present the concepts and metaphors in a way that hints at some of their subversive wealth, that I have captured some of their poetic and philosophical challenge to life and the prospective shape of life. This is why I have used the word poetics: a poetics of education, a poetics of culture. The concepts and metaphors are, emphatically, against the flow. I do not want them to become reified into further objects of knowledge, further items to transmit, to classify and to regurgitate within the current status quo. Because they are of another order of being, and invoke that order, that would be the final betrayal.

Notes

Introduction

1 Jean-Francois Lyotard (1984) *The Postmodern Condition: A Report on Knowledge*, trans. Geoff Bennington and Brian Massumi, Manchester, Manchester University Press, p. xxv.

2 Frederich Nietzsche (1989) *Beyond Good and Evil*, section 6. This translation made by Ronald Hayman and quoted in (1997) *Nietzsche*, London, Phoenix, p. 32. Later in the same passage Nietzsche claims: 'Nothing at all about the philosopher is impersonal; above all his morality provides decided and decisive evidence about *who he is*.'

1 The arts, postmodern culture and the inner dynamic of authentic education

1 Vaclav Havel (1961) *Between Past and Future*, London, Faber and Faber, pp. 154–155.

2 Alex's story was written as part of her autobiographical work on the MA *Language, Arts and Education* course at the University of Sussex. This course, designed to open up the aesthetic, ethical and creative elements in education, came to a close as the instrumental and managerial demands of the National Curriculum made themselves felt in the life of Education departments in our universities. Most of our Education departments are now confined to instrumental and managerial matters, a story of cultural depletion and ruthless survival with a numbing loss of meaning.

3 Ibid.

4 Elenchus is a key concept in Socratic pedagogy. It refers to that perplexity in understanding which is induced by the power of questioning. It is a seminal notion entirely antithetical to today's limited educational goals. For a fuller account of Socratic learning see my account 'The nature of Socratic learning' in (1994) *The Educational Imperative: A Defence of Socratic and Aesthetic Learning* London, Falmer Press.

5 Roger Scruton (1990) *The Philosopher on Dover Beach*, Manchester, Carcanet, pp. 44–45.

6 John Dewey (1981) *The Philosophy of John Dewey,* ed. John J. McDermott, Chicago, University of Chicago Press, p. 450.
7 Jean Baudrillard (1997) *The Post Modern History Reader,* ed. Keith Jenkins, London, Routledge, p. 40.
8 See Neil Postman (1985) *Amusing Ourselves to Death,* New York, Viking.
9 Aldous Huxley (1994) *Brave New World,* no page numbers given, London, Flamingo.
10 Hannah Arendt (1961) *Between Past and Future,* London, Faber and Faber, pp. 154–155.
11 For the full context see main feature article in the *Daily Telegraph,* 3 May 2002, p. 5.

2 On the spiritual in art, culture and education

1 This example is taken from the 1993 circular *Religious Education and Collective Worship* but it could as well be a circular for 2002 – the rhetoric does not change. The conceptions never seem to inform the whole gestalt of the curriculum, nor do they relate to any potential conflict with the surrounding consumer society. They are kept unproblematized and anodyne.
2 William Blake (1927) *Poetry and Prose of William Blake* ed. Geoffrey Keynes, London, Nonesuch Press, p. 582.
3 Ibid. p. 580.
4 Ibid. p. 580.
5 The exact words of William Blake were: 'The Old and New Testaments are the Great Code of Art', ibid. p. 582.
6 From a letter to Theo in (1963) *The Letters of Vincent Van Gogh,* ed. Mark Roskill, London, Fontana, p. 295.
7 Ibid. p. 286.
8 See W. Kandinsky (1997) *Concerning the Spiritual in Art,* New York, Dover. Here Kandinsky claims that the technical has ousted the metaphysical: 'The question "what?" disappears; only the question "how" remains . . . The method becomes a rationale. Art loses its soul', p. 28.
9 For a significant study opening up this theme see (1986) *The Spiritual in Art: Abstract Painting 1890–1985,* ed. Maurice Tuchman, New York, Abbeville Press.
10 From Max Beckmann's lecture *On My Painting* given in 1938 after he had moved to Amsterdam. It is quoted in William Bauress' doctoral thesis: *Max Beckmann and the Tradition of German Self Portraiture,* 29 April 1999, University of Sussex.
11 This is one of the great metaphysical poems of the nineteenth century. See (1965) *The Poems of Matthew Arnold* ed. Kenneth Allott, London, Longmans, pp. 239–243.
12 Shelley in a *Defence of Poetry* in *Essays and Letters of Percy Bysshe Shelley* with an introductory note by Ernest Rhys, London, Walter Scott Publishing, no date given, pp 16–17. It is pertinent that in his magnificent defence of poetry Shelley proposes: 'The cultivation of poetry is never more to be desired than at periods when, from an excess of the

selfish and calculating principle, the accumulation of the materials of external life exceed the quantity of the power of assimilating them to the internal laws of human nature.' It is an eloquent summary of part of the argument being put forward in this chapter.

13 This is a reference to Ludwig Wittgenstein's closing reflection in *Tractatus Logico-Philosophicus* where he writes: 'What we cannot speak about we must pass over in silence.' See (1961) *Tractatus Logico-Philosophicus* trans. Pears and McGuiness London, Routledge & Kegan Paul, p. 74. The assumption is that we speak about the world in propositional language and that is the only way of making sense, but the arts speak about our human world in non-propositional ways. What one cannot say in propositional words may be 'spoken' in art, dance, music, poetry etc.

14 James Boyd-White (2001) *The Edge of Meaning*, Chicago, IL, University of Chicago Press, p. 288. This is a most impressive recent volume on education in the broadest sense, the sympathetic study of meaning across a diversity of symbolic forms, from law to language, to painting and poetry. His own short autobiographical codas gave me considerable heart in the idea of opening each chapter of this book with a brief personal prelude, to connect the inner life to the outer, to attempt to disclose both.

15 Ibid.

16 A lively introduction to Hegel's notion of democracy, spirit and the consumer society can be found in Francis Fukayama (1992) *The End of History and The Last Man*, London, Penguin. The haunting idea of the end of history, also deriving from Hegel, is alluded to in my last chapter 'Art against the Zeitgeist'.

17 Don Cupitt (1997) *After God: The Future of Religion*, London, Weidenfeld and Nicolson, p. 120. Don Cupitt's contribution to a postmodern theology has been brilliant and tireless. Whether it can still be called Christianity is another matter.

18 Ibid.

19 I have adapted this list of principles from R. J. Hollingdale's perceptive introduction to his translation of Nietzsche's (1969) *Thus Spoke Zarathustra*, London Penguin. *Amor fati* refers, of course, to the creative affirmation of one's own fate even to the extent that one would want it, in all its contrary aspects, to happen again and again, to will it as part of the hypothesized pattern of eternal recurrence. For a working gloss on many of Nietzsche's key terms see the appendix to (1999) *Nietzsche and Postmodernism* by Dave Robinson, Cambridge, Icon Books.

20 Here the educational writings of David Holbrook remain relevant. See, for example, (1971) *Human Hope and the Death Instinct: An Exploration of Pyscho-analytical Theories of Human Nature and their Implications for Culture and Education*, London, Pergamon. More recently the writings of Christopher Bollas have advocated, with conviction, the development of creativity before life. See, for example, (2002) *Free Association*, Cambridge, Icon Books. It is this Goetheian idea of education as moral and imaginative growth which

has been so badly eclipsed under the reign of the operational imperative. A tragic loss to our culture and society.

3 The rise and fall of the new arts paradigm in education

1 See Thomas Kuhn (1970) *The Structure of Scientific Revolutions*, 2nd edition, Chicago, IL, University of Chicago Press, p. 85.
2 Quoted in Kuhn, ibid.
3 Malcolm Ross (1989) *The Claims of Feeling*, London, Falmer Press, p. 9.
4 Ibid.
5 Leslie Stratta (1972) 'Language and experience', *English Education* 3, (6), Autumn, p. 100.
6 Brian Way (1967) *Development through Drama*, London, Longman, p. 12.
7 Herbert Read (1943) *Education through Art*, 3rd edition, London, Faber and Faber, p. 200.
8 John Paynter and Peter Aston (1970) *Sound and Silence*, Cambridge, Cambridge University Press, p. 5.
9 Ibid. p. 7.
10 Robert Witkin (1974) *The Intelligence of Feeling*, London, Heinemann Educational Books, p. 126.
11 Malcolm Ross (1978) *The Creative Arts*, London, Heinemann Educational Books, p 48.
12 Max Beckmann quoted in Hans Belting (1989) *Tradition as Problem in Modern Art*, trans. Peter Wortsman, New York, Timken, p. 119.
13 Keith Swanwick and Dorothy Taylor (1982) *Discovering Music: Developing the Music Curriculum in Secondary Schools*, London, Batsford, pp. 124–125.
14 Edwin Webb in a personal communication to the author, dated 7 March, 2002. Edwin Webb is the author of (1991) *Literature and Education: Encounter and Experience*, London, Falmer Press.
15 Charles Plummeridge in a personal communication to the author, summer 2002. Charles Plummeridge is the author of (1991) *Music Education in Theory and Practice*, London, Falmer Press.
16 The concept of multiple intelligence was advocated by Howard Gardiner in 1993 in his influential volume *Frames of Mind: The Theory of Multiple Intelligences* (London, Fontana), a book that had a striking affinity with the arguments made in the *Falmer Press Library Of Aesthetic Education*.
17 Jean-François Lyotard (1984). See the introduction to *The Postmodern Condition: A Report on Knowledge*, Manchester, Manchester University Press, pxxv.

4 The three faces of wisdom

1 James Joyce (1986) *Ulysses*, the corrected text edited by Hans Walter Gabler with Wolfhard Steppe and Claus Melchior, Harmondsworth, Penguin, p. 34.

2 James Joyce in (1944) *Stephen Hero: Part of the first draft of 'A Portrait of the Artist as a Young Man'*, London, Jonathan Cape, p. 216. Later Stephen links epiphany to the recognition of the organized composite structure of a thing: 'finally, when the relation of the parts is exquisite, when the parts are adjusted to the special point, we recognize that it is *that* thing which it is. Its soul, its whatness, leaps to us from the vestment of its appearance. The soul of the commonest object, the structure of which is so adjusted, seems to us radiant. The object achieves its epiphany', p. 218.

3 James Joyce (1927), *James Joyce: a Portrait of the Artist as a Young Man, A facsimile of Epiphanies, Notes, Manuscripts and Typescripts* ed. Hans Walter Gabler, New York and London, Garland Publishing, p. 39.

4 Ibid. p. 46.

5 James Joyce (1914) *Dubliners*, London, Grant Richards, pp. 277–278.

6 Walter Pater quoted in (1972) *James Joyce's Early Fiction*, Homer Obed Brown, Cleveland and London, The Press of Case Western Reserve University, p. 130.

7 Ibid.

8 Emily Dickinson. Dickinson's poems generally did not have titles. Throughout the chapter the versions of the poems have been taken in their original form from *The Complete Poems of Emily Dickinson*, (1957) ed. Thomas Johnson, New York, Little Brown and Company. Earlier versions of Dickinson's work were notoriously subject to the intrusive hands of earnest and well-meaning critics. Early anthologies even deleted all the hyphens – so characteristic of her idiom – and inserted conventional punctuation. For the literary context see the introducion to *The Complete Poems of Emily Dickinson*.

9 Ibid.

10 Ibid.

11 Ibid.

12 Ibid.

13 Ibid.

14 Ibid.

15 William Blake, (1967) *Jerusalem* from the preface to *Milton* in *The Complete Poetry and Prose of William Blake*, London, Nonesuch Press, p. 375.

16 Ibid.

17 This is a very free 'personal' translation of Celan's poem taken from (1997) Peter Abbs *Angelic Imagination*, Lewes, Gryphon Press. It is, indeed, more a creative version than a translation. For the original and a more literal translation see (1996) Michael Hamburger *Paul Celan: Selected Poems*, Harmondsworth, Penguin.

5 The creative word and the creative life

1 Don Cupitt in (1998) *The Time Being*, London, SCM Press, p. 126.

2 See Michel Foucault (1970a) *The Order of Things: an Archaeology of the Human Sciences*, London, Tavistock.

3 Elias Canetti quoted in (1997) *The Post Modern History Reader*, ed. Keith Jenkins, London, Routledge, p. 39.
4 See John Burnett (1920) *Early Greek Philosophy*, London, A & C Black p. 139. All the fragments of Heraclitus are translated and presented in this early lucid study of pre-Socratic philosophy.
5 Ibid.
6 Jean Jacques Rousseau in (1959) *Oeuvres Completes: Les Confessions, Autres Textes Autobiographiques*, Paris, Editions Gallimard, p. 1148. Translated by Judith Keyston for the author.
7 Ibid. p. 1148.
8 Jean Jacques Rousseau in (1953) *The Confessions* trans. J. M. Cohen, London, Penguin, pp. 12–13.
9 Ibid.
10 See Carl Jung's (1963) *Memories, Dreams, Reflections* recorded and edited by Aniela Jaffé, London, Routledge and Kegan Paul. See, particularly, the glossary pp. 349–357 offering definitions of Jung's key concepts.
11 Cupitt (1998).
12 Ibid.
13 Roland Barthes (1977) *Roland Barthes by Roland Barthes* translated by Richard Howard, New York, Hill and Wang, p. 143.
14 L'ordre dont je ne me souviens plus: *the order I no longer remember*. Ibid. p. 148.
15 Ibid. p. 148.
16 Ibid.
17 Nouveau sujet, nouvelle science: *new subject, new science*. Ibid. p. 79.
18 Ibid.
19 Ibid. No page number given.
20 Ibid.
21 While working on this chapter a formidable new mapping of the story of autobiography has been published. It is the most comprehensive global survey so far. Readers interested in the history of the genre will find it an invaluable resource. See (2001) *Encyclopedia of Life Writing in Two Volumes*, ed. Margaretta Jolly, London and Chicago, IL, Fitzroy Dearborn.

6 Music, metaphor, meaning

1 Gerard Manley Hopkins quoted in (1978) *In Extremity; a Study of Gerard Manley Hopkins* by John Robinson, Cambridge, Cambridge University Press, p. 68. Chapter 3, 'Purging the Language', is a perceptive study of the perfomative nature of Hopkin's poetry.
2 Ibid.
3 In a letter to Robert Bridges dated 22 April 1879. Ibid. p. 69.
4 In a letter to Robert Bridges dated 18 October 1882. Ibid.
5 In a letter to Robert Bridges dated 11 December 1886. Ibid.
6 In a letter by Emily Dickinson quoted by Andrea Hollander Budy in *Resurgence* July/August 2001, No 207, p. 24.
7 These are the closing words of *The Waste Land* first published in 1923.

T. S. Eliot writes in his concluding note: '"Shantih". Repeated as here, a formal ending to an Upanishad, "The peace which passeth understanding" is our equivalent to this word.' *The Waste Land and Other Poems* (1951), London, Faber and Faber, p. 43.

8 From *The Waste Land*, ibid. pp. 42–43. The translation 'give, sympathize, control' is the one offered by Eliot himself in the notes to the poem, p. 50.

9 From *The Straitening* in (1996) *Paul Celan: Selected Poems* translated by Michael Hamburger, Harmondsworth, Penguin, p. 145. The introduction by Michael Hamburger provides a most lucid account of Celan's life and work.

10 Paul Celan, *Collected Prose* (1999) trans. Rosemarie Waldrop, Manchester, Carcanet, p. 17.

11 Ibid.

12 Rainer Maria Rilke (1960) *Selected Works, Volume 2 Poetry*, trans. J. B. Leishman, London, Hogarth Press, p. 354. I have used a different lineation. These words are inscribed on Rilke's tombstone in the churchyard at Raron near Muzot.

13 Rainer Maria Rilke, (1960) *Selected Prose, Volume 1*, trans. J. B. Leishman, Hogarth Press, p. 114.

14 See Paul Ricoeur (1978) *The Rule of Metaphor*, London, Routledge and Kegan Paul. A seminal book on the nature of metaphor.

7 Thirty-nine notes towards a new metaphysical poetry

1 From Euripides' (1919) *The Frogs*. See *The Frogs of Aristophanes* trans. Benjamin Rogers, London, G. Bell and Sons, p. 215.

2 Sappho Fragment 56 in a translation by Mary Barnard in (1996) *Sappho*, Berkeley and Los Angeles, CA, University of California Press, no page numbers.

3 Fragment 8 ibid.

4 Fragment 98 ibid.

5 Fragment 1 ibid.

6 Fragment 8 op cit.

7 This is a restatement of an earlier theme in the book. See note 13 to Chapter 2.

8 Op cit.

8 Art against the Zeitgeist

1 Calvin Tomkins (1997) *Duchamp*, London, Chatto and Windus, p. 464.

2 Quoted in (1999) *Marcel Duchamp* by Dawn Ades, Neil Cox and David Hopkins, London, Thames and Hudson, p. 211.

3 Hegel, (1993) *Introductory Lectures on Aesthetics*, ed. Michael Inwood, London, Penguin, pp. 12–13. Hegel concludes: 'Our present in its universal condition is not favourable to art.' He sees art petering out in reflection and irony – a stage already reached, he argued, in his own lifetime. Hegel died in 1831.

4 This satirical piece of verse by John Heath-Stubbs was quoted to me by one of my students. Perhaps it has become part of the oral tradition expressing a common sentiment?

5 Herbert Read in 'The limits of permissiveness' from (1975) *The Black Rainbow: Essays on the Present Breakdown of Culture* ed. by Peter Abbs, London, Heinemann Education Books, p. 5.

6 William Feaver in *The Observer*, Review section, December 1995.

7 Ibid.

8 This is the view expressed in the study *Marcel Duchamp*. Op cit. p. 189.

9 See Nietzsche (1968a) *The Will to Power* ed. and trans. Walter Kaufmann and R. J. Hollingdale, New York, Vintage Books (1967).

10 Shelagh Hourahane in a review published in *Planet*, No 142, August/September, 2000, pp. 119–120.

11 See Jacob Epstein (1963) *An Autobiography*, London, Vista Books.

12 John Meirion Morris in a personal communication to the author.

13 Anne Ross (1967) *Pagan Celtic Britain: Studies in Iconography and Tradition*, London, Routledge, p. 21.

14 John Meirion Morris in a personal communication to the author.

Bibliography

Abbs, P. (ed.) (1987) *Living Powers: The Arts in Education*, London, Falmer Press.

Abbs, P. (1988) *A is for Aesthetic: Essays on Creative and Aesthetic Education*, London, Falmer Press.

Abbs, P. (ed.) (1989) *The Symbolic Order: A Contemporary Reader on the Arts Debate*, London, Falmer Press.

Abbs, P. (1994) *The Educational Imperative: A Defence of Socratic and Aesthetic Learning*, London, Falmer Press.

Abbs, P. (1996) *The Polemics of Imagination*, London, Skoob Books.

Ades, D. *et al.* (1999) *Marcel Duchamp*, London, Thames and Hudson.

Arendt, H. (1961) *Between Past and Future*, London, Faber and Faber.

Bakhtin, M. M. (1981) *The Dialogic Imagination: Four Essays*, trans. M. Holquist and C. Emerson, Austin, TX, University of Texas Press.

Baudrillard, J. (1988) *Selected Writings*, ed. Mark Poster, Cambridge, Polity Press.

Best, D. (1990) *The Rationality of Feeling: The Arts in Education*, London, Falmer Press.

Bloom, H. (1994) *The Western Canon: The Books and School of the Ages*, London, Macmillan.

Bollas, C. (2002) *Free Association*, Cambridge, Icon Books.

Boyd-White, J. (2001) *The Edge of Meaning*, Chicago, IL, University of Chicago Press.

Brook, P. (1987) *The Shifting Point*, London, Harper & Row.

Broudy, H. (1972) *Enlightened Cherishing: An Essay on Aesthetic Education*, Chicago, IL, University of Illinois Press.

Cassirer, E. (1944) *An Essay on Man*, New York, Bantam Books.

Cassirer, E. (1955/8) *The Philosophy of Symbolic Forms* (three volumes) New Haven, CT, Yale University Press.

Collingwood, R. G. (1985) *The Principles of Art*, Oxford, Oxford University Press.

Cupitt, D. (1984) *The Sea of Faith*, London, BBC.

Cupitt, D. (1997) *After God: The Future of Religion*, London, Weidenfeld and Nicolson.

Danto, A. (1987) *The State of the Art*, New Jersey, Prentice Hall.

Dewey, J. (1934) *Art as Experience*, New York, Minton Balch & Company.

Docherty, T. (ed.) (1993) *Postmodernism: A Reader*, Hemel Hempstead, Harvester Wheatsheaf.

Donoghue, D. (1985) *The Arts Without Mystery*, London, BBC.

Eagleton, T. (1983) *Literary Theory*, Oxford, Basil Blackwell.

Eagleton, T. (1990) *The Ideology of the Aesthetic*, Oxford, Basil Blackwell.

Eliot, T.S. (1975) *Selected Prose of T.S. Eliot*, ed. Frank Kermode, London, Faber & Faber.

Falck, C. (1999) *Myth, Truth and Literature: Towards a True Post-Modernity*, Cambridge, Cambridge University Press.

Foucault, M. (1970a) *The Order of Things: An Archeology of the Human Sciences*, London, Tavistock.

Foucault, M. (1970b) *The History of Sexuality*, (three volumes) Harmondsworth, Penguin.

Freud, S. (1973a) *Introductory Lectures on Psychoanalysis*, Harmondsworth, Penguin.

Freud, S. (1973b) *New Introductory Lectures on Psychoanalysis*, Harmondsworth, Penguin.

Frye, N. (1957) *The Anatomy of Criticism*, Princeton, NJ, Princeton University Press.

Fuller, P. (1980a) *Art and Psychoanalysis*, London, Writers & Readers.

Fuller, P. (1980b) *Beyond the Crisis in Art*, London, Writer & Readers.

Fuller, P. (1982) *Aesthetics after Modernism*, London, Writers & Readers.

Fuller, P. (1985) *Images of God*, London, Chatto & Windus.

Fuller, P. (1988) *Theoria*, London, Chatto & Windus.

Fukayama, F. (1992) *The End of History and the Last Man*, London, Penguin.

Gibson, R. (1986) *Structuralism and Education*, Oxford, Pergamon.

Gombrich, E. (1966) *Norm and Form*, Oxford, Phaidon.

Gombrich, E. (1978) *The Story of Art*, Oxford, Phaidon.

Gombrich, E. (1979) *The Sense of Order*, Oxford, Phaidon.

Gombrich, E. (1984) *Tributes: Interpreters of our Cultural Tradition*, Oxford, Phaidon.

Gombrich, E. (1986) *Art and Illusion*, Oxford, Phaidon.

Greene, M. (1988) *The Dialectic of Freedom*, New York, Teachers College Press.

Hamburger, M. (1989) *Testimonies: Selected Shorter Prose*, Manchester, Carcanet.

Havel, V. (1987) *Living in Truth*, London, Faber & Faber.

Havelock, E. (1963) *Preface to Plato*, Cambridge, MA, Harvard University Press.

Hayman, R. (1997) *Neitzsche*, London, Phoenix.

Hegel, W. F. (1993) *Introductory Lectures on Aesthetics*, ed. Michael Inwood, Harmondsworth, Penguin.

Hughes, T. (1994) 'Myth and education' in *The Symbolic Order*, ed. Peter Abbs, London, Falmer Press.

Hutcheon, L. (1988) *A Poetics of Postmodernism: History, Theory, Fiction*, London, Routledge.

Hutcheon, L. (1989) *The Politics of Postmodernism*, London, Routledge.

Jenks, C. (1993) 'The Emergent Rules' in *Postmodernism: A Reader*, ed. Tomas Docherty, Hemel Hempstead, Harvester Wheatsheaf.

Jenks, C. (1997) *The Language of Post-Modern Architecture*, London, Academy Editions.

Jolly, M. (2001) *Encyclopedia of Life Writing*, (two volumes) London and Chicago, IL, Fitzroy Dearborn.

Jung, C. (1959) *The Archetypes and the Collective Unconscious*, London, Routledge and Kegan Paul.

Jung, C. (1963) *Memories, Dreams, Reflections*, London, Collins and Routledge & Kegan Paul.

Jung, C. *et al.* (1964) *Man and His Symbols*, London, Aldus Books.

Kandinsky, W. (1977) *Concerning the Spiritual in Art*, trans. M. T. H. Sadler, New York, Dover Publications.

Kant, I. (1987) *Critique of Judgment*, trans. Werner S. Pluhar, Indianapolis, IN, Hackett Publishing.

Knights, L. C. (1960) *Selected Essays in Criticism*, London, Chatto & Windus.

Koestler, A. (1975) *The Act of Creation*, London, Picador.

Kuhn, T. (1970) *The Structure of Scientific Revolutions*, Chicago, IL, University of Chicago Press.

Langer, S. (1953) *Feeling and Form*, London, Routledge & Kegan Paul.

Langer, S. (1957a) *Philosophy in a New Key*, Cambridge, MA, Harvard University Press.

Langer, S. (1957b) *Problems of Art*, London, Routledge & Kegan Paul.

Langer, S. (1974) *Mind: An Essay on Human Feeling*, Baltimore, MO, Johns Hopkins University Press.

Leiter, B. (2002) *Nietzsche on Morality*, London, Routledge.

Lipman, M. (ed.) (1973) *Contemporary Aesthetics*, Boston, MA, Allyn & Bacon.

Lodge, D. (1981) *Working with Structuralism*, London, Routledge & Kegan Paul.

Lyotard, J.-F. (1984) *The Postmodern Condition: A Report on Knowledge*, trans. Geoff Bennington and Brian Massumi, Manchester, Manchester University Press.

Marcuse, H. (1978) *The Aesthetic Dimension*, London, Macmillan.

Mordaunt Crook, J. (1987) *The Dilemma of Style*, London, John Murray.

Mumford, L. (1971) *The Myth of the Machine*, London, Secker & Warburg.

Murdoch, I. (1992) *Metaphysics as a Guide to Morals*, London, Chatto & Windus.

Nietzsche, F. (1968a) *The Will to Power*, trans. Walter Kaufmann and R. J. Hollingdale, New York, Vintage.

Nietzsche, F. (1968b) *The Twilight of the Idols* and *The Anti-Christ*, trans. R. J. Hollingdale, New York, Penguin Books.

Nietzsche, F. (1980) 'On truth and lie in an extra-moral sense', in *The Portable Nietzsche*, ed. Walter Kaufmann, New York, Random House.

Nietzsche, F. (1989) *Beyond Good and Evil: Prelude to a Philosophy of the Future*, trans. Walter Kaufmann, New York, Vintage.

Norris, C. (1990) *What's Wrong with Postmodernism*, Hemel Hempstead, Harvester Wheatsheaf.

Oakshott, M. (1989) *The Voice of Liberal Learning*, New Haven, CT and London, Yale University Press.

Olney, J. (1972) *Metaphors of the Self*, Princeton, NJ, Princeton University Press.

Olney, J. (1980) *Autobiography: Essays Theoretical and Critical*, Princeton, NJ, Princeton University Press.

Otto, R. (1925) *The Idea of the Holy*, trans. John W. Harvey, Oxford, Oxford University Press.

Phenix, P. (1964) *Realms of Meaning*, New York, McGraw Hill.

Polanyi, M. (1973) *Personal Knowledge*, London, Routledge & Kegan Paul.

Postman, N. (1985) *Amusing Ourselves to Death*, New York, Viking.

Read, H. (1943) *Education through Art*, London, Faber & Faber.

Read, H. (1955) *Ikon and Idea*, London, Faber & Faber.

Redfern, H. B. (1986) *Questions in Aesthetic Education*, London, Allen & Unwin.

Reid, L. A. (1961) *Ways of Knowledge and Experience*, London, Allen & Unwin.

Reid, L. A. (1970) *Meaning in the Arts*, London, Allen & Unwin.

Reid, L. A. (1986) *Ways of Understanding and Education*, London, Heinemann Educational Books.

Ricoeur, P. (1978) *The Rule of Metaphor: Multi-Disciplinary Studies of the Creation of Meaning in Language*, trans. Robert Czerny, London, Routledge and Kegan Paul.

Robinson, D. (1999) *Nietzsche and Postmodernism*, Cambridge, Icon Books.

Robinson, J. (1978) *In Extremity: A Study of Gerard Manley Hopkins*, Cambridge, Cambridge University Press.

Ross, M. (1989) *The Creative Arts*, London, Heinemann Educational Books.

Schiller, F. (1974) *On the Aesthetic Education of Man*, Oxford, Clarendon Press.

Scruton, R. (1974) *Art and Imagination*, London, Methuen.

Scruton, R. (1979) *The Aesthetics of Architecture*, London, Methuen.

Scruton, R. (1983) *The Aesthetic Understanding*, London, Methuen.

Scruton, R. (1990) *The Philosopher on Dover Beach*, Manchester, Carcanet.

Small, C. (1977) *Music, Society, Education*, London, John Calder.

Smith, R. and Simpson, A. (1991) *Aesthetics and Arts Education*, Chicago, IL, University of Illinois Press.

Steiner, G. (1967) *Real Presences*, Harmondsworth, Penguin.

Steiner, G. (1975) *After Babel*, Cambridge, Cambridge University Press.

Steiner, G. (2001) *Grammars of Creation*, London, Faber & Faber.

Stokes, A. (1965) *The Invitation in Art*, London, Tavistock.

Storr, A. (1972) *Dynamics of Creation*, London, Penguin.

Tarnas, R. (1991) *The Passion of the Western Mind*, London, Pimlico.

Taylor, C. (1989) *Sources of the Self*, Cambridge, Cambridge University Press.

Tippett, M. (1974) *Moving into Aquarius*, London, Picador.

Tomkins, C. (1997) *Duchamp*, London, Chatto and Windus.

Valery, P. (1964) *Aesthetics*, London, Routledge & Kegan Paul.

Warnock, M. (1980) *Imagination*, London, Faber & Faber.

Whalley, G. (1953) *Poetic Process*, Chicago, IL, Greenwood Press.

Winnicot, D. W. (1971) *Playing and Reality*, London, Tavistock.

Witkin, R. (1974) *The Intelligence of Feeling*, London, Heinemann Educational Books.

Wittgenstein, L. (1966) *Lectures and Conversations on Aesthetics, Psychology and Religious Belief*, Oxford, Oxford University Press.

Wollheim, R. (1970) *Art and Its Objects: An Introduction to Aesthetics*, London, Harper & Row.

Index